LOCKE

Plain Texts from Key Thinkers

Edited by Anthony Kelbrook

PARMA BOOKS, LONDON

First edition 1997

Copyright © Parma Books

ISBN 1-901678-059

Published by Parma Books,
99 Wallis Road, London, E9 5LN

Printed in Great Britain by
Antony Rowe, Chippenham, Wiltshire

Locke

CONTENTS

INTRODUCTION

(a) Political Writings:

Locke's political writings are a sustained case for the doctrine expressed in the United States Declaration of Independence that legitimate political power rests on the consent of the governed. Governments, he claims, are formed by men in a state of nature who come together to form a political society for their better protection and especially for the better protection of their property. Locke imagines the state of nature as governed by "natural law." This was a common concept in the seventeenth century and was conceived as some fundamental principles of morality evident to every individual. In the state of Nature each man must be the defender of his own rights or property. In political society he puts their protection in the hands of others. A standard, much argued question, is whether the emergence of political society from the state of nature should be looked on as an actual historical event or simply as a way of looking at matters which serves to clarify the nature of political society. The notion of the emergence of government by the agreement of men previously in a state of nature corresponds well to the wording of the United States Declaration of Independence, "We hold these truths to be self evident that all men are born equal and invested by their creator with certain inalienable rights, . . . that to attain these ends governments are instituted among men, deriving their just powers from the consent of the governed."

The Texts:

The texts of political philosophy reproduced here are all chapters from the *Second Treatise on Government*. The first "Of the Beginning of Political Societies" opens with the following ringing statement that government rests on the consent of the governed,

"Men being as has been said by nature all free, equal and independent, no man can be put out of this estate and subjected to the political power of another without his own consent" the only way that consent is given is by "...agreeing with other men to join and unite into a community for their comfortable, safe and peaceable living one amongst another is a secure enjoyment of their properties, and a greater security against those that are not of it" Shortly afterwards he goes on:

"For when any number of men have, by the consent of every individual, made a community, they have thereby made that community one body, with a power to act as one body, which is only by the will and determination of the majority." The rest of the chapter consists in a discussion of two possible objections to his position. These are stated in s. 100.

"Of the Ends of Political Society and Government" considers the purposes ("ends") with which governments are formed. We are told, "The great and chief end therefore of men's uniting into Commonwealths and putting themselves under governments, is the preservation of their property, to which in the state of nature there are many things wanting" Locke concludes by noting that having been founded for this purpose governments must be "directed to no other end but the peace, safety and public good of the people".

In the next chapter "Of the Forms of a Commonwealth" he discusses the different forms which such a government can take. Despite his earlier talk of the majority he does not conclude that such governments must be democracies in the modern sense. he accepts that this majority may choose to place political power in the hands of an "oligarchy" or monarchy.

"Of the Extent of the Legislative Power" goes into greater detail on the limits of government power. In his first and second points he notes that it must not be "arbitrary" Third, governments may not confiscate property and lastly "the legislative cannot transfer the power of making laws into any other hands"

"Of the Legislative, Executive and Federative Power of the Commonwealth" recommends, for prudence a separation of the law making ("legislative") powers and of "executive" powers relating to the application or enforcement of the law, "... because it may be too great a temptation to human frailty, apt to grasp at power to execute them, whereby they may exempt themselves from obedience to the laws they make."

The chapter "Of the Subordination of the Powers of the Commonwealth" maintains that "there remains still in the people a supreme power to remove or alter the legislative when they find the legislative act contrary to the trust reposed in them." He goes on to discuss and present as legitimate the possible role of the executive in calling and dissolving the legislature.

In the later chapter "On Tyranny," the last reproduced here, Locke develops the last theme and makes explicit the right of the people to rebel against unjust government. "And whosoever in authority exceeds the power given him by the law, and makes use of the force he has under his command to compass that upon the subject which the law allows not, ceases in that to be a magistrate, [a term used her to cover anybody acting with lawful authority] and, acting without authority, may be opposed, as any other man who by force invades the rights of another." Here we are once more in the territory of the Declaration of Independence.

(b) *Locke's Theory of Knowledge*

The *Essay Concerning Human Understanding,* from which all the texts reproduced here are taken, is an attempt to determine how the mind is capable of obtaining knowledge of the world. Although much more a matter of what is sometimes called technical philosophy such an enquiry still has links with the political philosophy. For example any writer who attributes or denies a role to authority, or to society and culture may well be making a point with political implications. Analogies with Locke's political philosophy are a subject to which we shall return at the end.

The model he proposes has in outline the advantage of simplicity. We have simple ideas such as colour, sound and so forth, these are the simple ideas of sensation. To them can be added simple ideas from reflection, that is from self consciousness, from the mind's awareness of itself. An example is the simple idea of thinking. Out of these are constructed complex ideas such as beauty or gratitude. Underlying this system is a strict insistence put forward in the first chapter of the essay, reproduced here, that there are no "innate principles" and hence that all knowledge is derived from experience. There is no inborn knowledge. Here Locke appears to be opposing Descartes who argued that the idea of God was innate i.e. that it was an idea implanted in the mind at birth which would in some way come into our thoughts regardless of experience or upbringing. It is interesting to notice that in taking this position Locke is also taking sides in a contemporary debate, for the notion of innate ideas has received fresh impetus in recent years from the work in linguistics of Noam Chomsky. The latter has suggested that the grammars of all languages share certain general characteristics and that a child learning to speak will be assisted by knowledge of these characteristics. The child, argues Chomsky will be aware that the grammar he is trying to learn cannot be just any system of rules but a system of rules of a particular kind. In this way, when the child attempts to discover the rules of grammar in the language he hears his task will be made easier because the search will be narrowed. Chomsky has gone on to generalise from this to suggest that all our perceptions interpret experience in ways determined by innate principles. He has even speculated on the possibility of devising a social and political system ideally suited to the supposed innate structure of the human mind. This is mentioned to show that Locke's writings do have a place in continuing and important controversies.

The Texts:

Locke's argument in his opening chapter, "No innate speculative principles" is tortuous and arguably somewhat repetitious. The chapter is reproduced in full here because it is so fundamental to his main theme that all knowledge comes from experience but, provided its main points are understood, the student fresh to Locke's work can be forgiven for not following every twist and turn of the argument.

At section four Locke takes two examples of possibly innate principles which he refers to as "maxims" These are "What is, is" and "It is impossible for the same thing to be and not to be." He makes constant reference to these throughout the rest of the chapter.   He attacks first (section two) the claim that general or universal assent to a principle shows it to be innate. First, (section three) assent could be explained on other grounds. Secondly, (section four) principles of the kind in question do not in any case achieve universal consent. Children, for example, on the contrary "have not the least apprehension or thought of them"

At section six he raises a possible counter argument: that people may come to realise these truths when they come to the age of reason. He replies first that, "If reason discovered these truths that would not prove them innate". For example the whole of mathematics could be deduced by reasoning but is not regarded as innately known to the mind. (If only, Locke could have said, because mathematics has developed slowly over centuries and so cannot be considered as known in its entirety to every human being at birth.) Moreover it cannot be suggested that these truths are discovered by reason. They are, to paraphrase Locke, too fundamental to rationality to require demonstration by reason. "For all reason is search, and casting about and requires pains and application. And how can it with any tolerable sense be supposed that what was imprinted by nature [ie: innate] as the foundation and guide of reason, should need the use of reason to discover it?" He argues in the next few sections that knowledge of such truths does not necessarily arrive at the age of reason. It cannot come before but may not come until later. In this they are no different from "other knowable truths" (section thirteen).

Throughout the next series of excerpts Locke classifies "simple ideas" (and his examples illustrate what he means by "simple idea") There are those derived solely from sensation, such as solidity "which arises from the resistance which we find in body, to the entrance of any other body into the place it possesses". Another category consists in ideas which derive from more than one sense. Examples are space, extension, figure, rest and motion. "For these make perceivable impressions both on the eye and on touch". Next come ideas "of reflection." These arise from the mind's own awareness of itself, "when it turns its view inward upon itself" Thinking is a simple, intuitively clear example, Lastly come "simple ideas of both sensation and reflection" An example is pleasure.

The next chapter reproduced here is "Some further considerations concerning our Simple Ideas of Sensation." Here he maintains that "simple ideas" are distinct from what gives rise to them. For example the idea of black corresponds simply to an absence of light, rest is absence of motion but whereas the corresponding reality consists simply in the lack of something the ideas are still "distinct positive ideas". this is the point at which Locke's realism emerges. He distinguishes between "our ideas" and the corresponding "qualities of bodies" and mention of qualities of bodies is an unambiguous assertion that there is a reality outside the mind. Here he avoids a line of argument taken by his successors in the British empirical tradition, Berkeley and Hume who both called into question the reality of matter. He avoids saying, as some philosophers have done, that our experience or reality is not fundamentally different from a dream. The subject of "qualities of bodies" leads to his famous distinction between "primary" and "secondary" qualities. The first are those such as "solidity, extension, figure and mobility" which are "utterly inseparable from the body in whatsoever state it be." Secondary qualities are the "power" of bodies to produce sensations in the mind. He attributes this power to the primary qualities, shape and so on of the microscopic parts. (There is a third, less important, kind of quality mentioned, for example "the power in fire to produce a new colour or consistency in wax or clay.")

The next chapter reproduced here is that "Of Complex Ideas". These are "made by the mind out of simple ones" by "combining several simple ideas into compound ones." he gives as examples: "beauty, gratitude, a man an army, the universe." They all fall under one of three categories: modes, substances and relations. The first, modes, are "not capable of subsisting by themselves" but are "dependencies on or affections of substances" for example "triangle gratitude, murder etc." The second, substances, are such combinations of simple ideas as are taken to represent "distinct particular things subsisting by themselves." In colloquial modern English one could convey Locke's meaning simply by saying that they are things. he gives as an example a man or a sheep, or "several of these put together, for example an army of men a flock of sheep." the last, relation, consideration and comparing one idea with another. No example is given in the chapter, but he later provides the examples of identity and diversity.

Locke's system has an overriding aim. It is a systematic attempt to show how all knowledge arises out of simple experience. The spirit is that which has given rise to modern science: of trusting in the last resort nothing but experience or experiment.

Lastly we must return to a subject touched on already, the relation of Locke's political philosophy and his theory of knowledge. The division both of this book and of this introduction might suggest that they belong to hermetically sealed compartments. There is however one respect in which they complement each other. Both are highly individualistic. Knowledge rests on the experience of the individual mind and political society rests on the desire of a number of individuals to protect their property. There is no discussion of how both individual personality and individual knowledge of the world may themselves be shaped by wider cultures and communities and it is arguably in this respect that Locke's philosophy is most vulnerable to criticism.

Of the Beginning of Political Societies.

95. Men being, as has been said, by nature, all free, equal, and independent, no one can be put out of this estate, and subjected to the political power of another, without his own consent. The only way whereby any one divests himself of his natural liberty, and puts on the bonds of civil society, is by agreeing with other men to join and unite into a community for their comfortable, safe, and peaceable living one amongst another, in a secure enjoyment of their properties, and a greater security against any, that are not of it. This any number of men may do, because it injures not the freedom of the rest; they are left as they were in the liberty of the state of nature. When any number of men have so consented to make one community or government, they are thereby presently incorporated, and make one body politic, wherein the majority have a right to act and conclude the rest.

96. For when any number of men have, by the consent of every individual, made a community, they have thereby made that community one body, with a power to act as one body, which is only by the will and determination of the majority: for that which acts any community, being only the consent of the individuals of it, and it being necessary to that which is one body to move one way; it is necessary the body should move that way whither the greater force carries it, which is the consent of the majority: or else it is impossible it should act or continue one body, one community, which the consent of every individual that united into it, agreed that it should; and so every one is bound by that consent to be concluded by the majority. And therefore we see, that in assemblies, empowered to act by positive laws, where no number is set by that positive law which empowers them, the act of the majority passes for the act of the whole, and of course determines, as having, by the law of nature and reason, the power of the whole.

97. And thus every man, by consenting with others to make one body politic under one government, puts himself under an obligation, to every one of that society, to submit to the determination of the majority, and to be concluded by it; or else this original compact, whereby he with others incorporates into one society, would signify nothing, and be no compact, if he be left free, and under no other ties than he was in before in the state of nature. For what appearance

would there be of any compact? what new engagement if he were no farther tied by any decrees of the society, than he himself thought fit, and did actually consent to? This would be still as great a liberty, as he himself had before his compact, or any one else in the state of nature hath, who may submit himself, and consent to any acts of it if he thinks fit.

98. For if the consent of the majority shall not, in reason, be received as the act of the whole, and conclude every individual; nothing but the consent of every individual can make any thing to be the act of the whole: but such a consent is next to impossible ever to be had, if we consider the infirmities of health, and avocations of business, which in a number, though much less than that of a commonwealth, will necessarily keep many away from the public assembly. To which if we add the variety of opinions, and contrariety of interests, which unavoidably happen in all collections of men, the coming into society upon such terms would be only like Cato's coming into the theatre, only to go out again. Such a constitution as this would make the mighty Leviathan of a shorter duration, than the feeblest creatures, and not let it outlast the day it was born in: which cannot be supposed, till we can think, that rational creatures should desire and constitute societies only to be dissolved: for where the majority cannot conclude the rest, there they cannot act as one body, and consequently will be immediately dissolved again.

99. Whosoever therefore out of a state of nature unite into a community, must be understood to give up all the power, necessary to the ends for which they unite into society, to the majority of the community, unless they expressly agreed in any number greater than the majority. And this is done by barely agreeing to unite into one political society, which is all the compact that is, or needs be, between the individuals, that enter into, or make up a commonwealth. And thus that, which begins and actually constitutes any political society, is nothing but the consent of any number of freemen capable of a majority to unite and incorporate into such a society. And this is that, and that only, which did, or could give beginning to any lawful government in the world.

100. To this I find two objections made.

First, That there are no instances to be found in story, of a company of men independent, and equal one amongst another, that met together, and in this way began and set up a government.

Secondly, It is impossible of right, that men should do so, because all men being born under government, they are to submit to that, and are not at liberty to begin a new one.

101. To the first there is this to answer, That it is not at all to be wondered, that history gives us but a very little account of men, that lived together in the state of nature. The inconveniences of that condition, and the love and want of society, no sooner brought any number of them together, but they presently united and incorporated, if they designed to continue together. And if we may not suppose men ever to have been in the state of nature, because we hear not much of them in such a state, we may as well suppose the armies of Salmanasser or Xerxes were never children, because we hear little of them, till they were men, and embodied in armies. Government is everywhere antecedent to records, and letters seldom come in amongst a people till a long continuation of civil society has, by other more necessary arts, provided for their safety, ease, and plenty: and then they begin to look after the history of their founders, and search into their original, when they have outlived the memory of it: for it is with commonwealths as with particular persons, they are commonly ignorant of their own births and infancies: and if they know any thing of their original, they are beholden for it, to the accidental records that others have kept of it. And those that we have, of the beginning of any polities in the world, excepting that of the Jews, where God himself immediately interposed, and which favours not at all paternal dominion, are all either plain instances of such a beginning as I have mentioned, or at least have manifest footsteps of it.

102. He must show a strange inclination to deny evident matter of fact, when it agrees not with his hypothesis, who will not allow, that show a strange inclination to deny evident matter of fact, when it agrees not with his hypothesis, who will not allow, that the beginning of Rome and Venice were by the uniting together of several men free and independent one of another, amongst whom there was no natural superiority or subjection. And if Josephus Acosta's word may be taken, he tells us, that in many parts of America there was no government at all. There are great and apparent conjectures, says he,

that these men, speaking of those of Peru, for a long time had neither kings nor commonwealths, but lived in troops, as they do this day in Florida, the Cheriquanas, those of Brazil, and many other nations, which have no certain kings, but as occasion is offered, in peace or war, they choose their captains as they please. If it be said, that every man there was born subject to his father, or the head of his family; that the subjection due from a child to a father took not away his freedom of uniting into what political society he thought fit, has been already proved. But be that as it will, these men, it is evident, were actually free; and whatever superiority some politicians now would place in any of them, they themselves claimed it not, but by consent were all equal, till by the same consent they set rulers over themselves. So that their politic societies all began from a voluntary union, and the mutual agreement of men freely acting in the choice of their governors, and forms of government.

103. And I hope those who went away from Sparta with Palantus, mentioned by Justin, will be allowed to have been freemen independent one of another, and to have set up a government over themselves, by their own consent. Thus I have given several examples, out of history, of people free and in the state of nature, that being met together incorporated and began a commonwealth. And if the want of such instances be an argument to prove that government were not, nor could not be so begun, I suppose the contenders for paternal empire were better let it alone, than urge it against natural liberty: for if they can give so many instances, out of history, of governments begun upon paternal right, I think (though at best an argument from what has been, to what should of right be, has no great force) one might, without any great danger, yield them the cause. But if I might advise them in the case, they would do well not to search too much into the original of governments, as they have begun de facto, lest they should find, at the foundation of most of them, something very little favourable to the design they promote, and such a power as they contend for.

104. But to conclude, reason being plain on our side, that men are naturally free, and the examples of history showing, that the governments of the world, that were begun in peace, had their beginning laid on that foundation, and were made by the consent of the people; there can be little room for doubt, either where the right is, or

what has been the opinion, or practice of mankind, about the first erecting of governments.

105. I will not deny, that if we look back as far as history will direct us, towards the original of commonwealths, we shall generally find them under the government and administration of one man. And I am also apt to believe, that where a family was numerous enough to subsist by itself, and continued entire together, without mixing with others, as it often happens, where there is much land, and few people, the government commonly began in the father: for the father having, by the law of nature, the same power with every man else to punish, as he thought fit, any offences against that law, might thereby punish his transgressing children, even when they were men, and out of their pupilage; and they were very likely to submit to his punishment, and all join with him against the offender, in their turns, giving him thereby power to execute his sentence against any transgression, and so in effect make him the law-maker, and governor over all that remained in conjunction with his family. He was fittest to be trusted; paternal affection secured their property and interest under his care; and the custom of obeying him, in their childhood, made it easier to submit to him, rather than to any other. If therefore they must have one to rule them, as government is hardly to be avoided amongst men that live together; who so likely to be the man as he that was their common father; unless negligence, cruelty, or any other defect of mind or body made him unfit for it? But when either the father died, and left his next heir, for want of age, wisdom, courage, or any other qualities, less fit for rule; or where several families met, and consented to continue together; there, it is not to be doubted, but they used their natural freedom, to set up him, whom they judged the ablest, and most likely, to rule well over them. Conformable hereunto we find the people of America, who (living out of the reach of the conquering swords, and spreading domination of the two great empires of Peru and Mexico) enjoyed their own natural freedom, though, *caeteris paribus*, [other things being equal] they commonly prefer the heir of their deceased king; yet if they find him any way weak, or incapable, they pass him by, and set up the stoutest and bravest man for their ruler.

106. Thus, though looking back as far as records give us any account of peopling the world, and the history of nations, we commonly find the government to be in one hand; yet it destroys not

that which I affirm, viz. that the beginning of politic society depends upon the consent of the individuals, to join into, and make one society; who, when they are thus incorporated, might set up what form of government they thought fit. But this having given occasion to men to mistake, and think, that by nature government was monarchical, and belonged to the father, it may not be amiss here to consider, why people in the beginning generally pitched upon this form, which though perhaps the father's pre-eminency might, in the first institution of some commonwealths, give a rise to, and place in the beginning, the power in one hand; yet it is plain that the reason, that continued the form of government in a single person, was not any regard, or respect to paternal authority; since all petty monarchies, that is, almost all monarchies, near their original, have been commonly, at least upon occasion, elective.

107. First then, in the beginning of things, the father's government of the childhood of those sprung from him, having accustomed them to the rule of one man, and taught them that where it was exercised with care and skill, with affection and love to those under it, it was sufficient to procure and preserve to men all the political happiness they sought for in society. It was no wonder that they should pitch upon, and naturally run into that form of government, which from their infancy they had been all accustomed to; and which, by experience, they had found both easy and safe. To which, if we add, that monarchy being simple, and most obvious to men, whom neither experience had instructed in forms of government, nor the ambition or insolence of empire had taught to beware of the encroachments of prerogative, or the inconveniences of absolute power, which monarchy in succession was apt to lay claim to, and bring upon them, it was not at all strange, that they should not much trouble themselves to think of methods of restraining any exorbitances of those to whom they had given the authority over them, and of balancing the power of government, by placing several parts of it in different hands. They had neither felt the oppression of tyrannical dominion, nor did the fashion of the age, nor their possessions, or way of living, (which afforded little matter for covetousness or ambition) give them any reason to apprehend or provide against it; and therefore it is no wonder they put themselves into such a frame of government, as was not only, as I said, most obvious and simple, but also best suited to their present state and

condition; which stood more in need of defence against foreign invasions and injuries, than of multiplicity of laws. The equality of a simple poor way of living, confining their desires within the narrow bounds of each man's small property, made few controversies, and so no need of many laws to decide them, or variety of officers to superintend the process, or look after the execution of justice, where there were but few trespasses, and few offenders. Since then those, who like one another so well as to join into society, cannot but be supposed to have some acquaintance and friendship together, and some trust one in another; they could not but have greater apprehensions of others, than of one another: and therefore their first care and thought cannot but be supposed to be, how to secure themselves against foreign force. It was natural for them to put themselves under a frame of government which might best serve to that end, and choose the wisest and bravest man to conduct them in their wars, and lead them out against their enemies, and in this chiefly be their ruler.

108. Thus we see, that the kings of the Indians in America, which is still a pattern of the first ages in Asia and Europe, whilst the inhabitants were too few for the country, and want of people and money gave men no temptation to enlarge their possessions of land, or contest for wider extent of ground, are little more than generals of their armies; and though they command absolutely in war, yet at home and in time of peace they exercise very little dominion, and have but a very moderate sovereignty, the resolutions of peace and war being ordinarily either in the people, or in a council. Though' the war itself, which admits not of plurality of governors, naturally devolves the command into the king's sole authority.

109. And thus in Israel itself, the chief business of their judges, and first kings, seems to have been to be captains in war, and leaders of their armies; which (besides what is signified by going out and in before the people, which was, to march forth to war, and home again in the heads of their forces) appears plainly in the story of Jephtha. The Ammonites making war upon Israel, the Gileadites in fear send to Jephtha, a bastard of their family whom they had cast off, and article with him, if he will assist them against the Ammonites, to make him their ruler; which they do in these words, And the people made him head and captain over them, (Judg. xi, ii) which was, as it seems, all

one as to be judge. And he judged Israel, (Judg. xii, 7) that is, was their captain-general six years. So when Jotham upbraids the Shechemites with the obligation they had to Gideon, who had been their judge and ruler, he tells them, He fought for you, and adventured his life far, and delivered you out of the hands of Midian, (Judg. ix, 17) Nothing mentioned of him but what he did as a general: and indeed that is all is found in his history, or in any of the rest of the judges. And Abimelech particularly is called king, though at most he was but their general. And when, being weary of the ill conduct of Samuel's sons, the children of Israel desired a king, like all the nations to judge them, and to go out before them, and to fight their battles, (I. Sam viii. 20) God granting their desire, says to Samuel, I will send thee a man, and thou shalt anoint him to be captain over my people Israel, that he may save my people out of the hands of the Philistines, (ix. 16) As if the only business of a king had been to lead out their armies, and fight in their defence; and accordingly at his inauguration pouring a vial of oil upon him, declares to Saul, that the Lord had anointed him to be captain over his inheritance, (x. 1) And therefore those, who after Saul's being solemnly chosen and saluted king by the tribes at Mispah, were unwilling to have him their king, made no other objection but this, How shall this man save us? (v. 27) as if they should have said, this man is unfit to be our king, not having skill and conduct enough in war, to be able to defend us. And when God resolved to transfer the government to David, it is in these words, But now thy kingdom shall not continue: the Lord hath sought him a man after his own heart, and the Lord hath commanded him to be captain over his people, (xiii. 14) As if the whole kingly authority were nothing else but to be their general: and therefore the tribes who had stuck to Saul's family, and opposed David's reign, when they came to Hebron with terms of submission to him, they tell him, amongst other arguments they had to submit to him as to their king, that he was in effect their king in Saul's time, and therefore they had no reason but to receive him as their king now. Also (say they) in time past, when Saul was king over us, thou wast he that reddest out and broughtest in Israel, and the Lord said unto thee, Thou shalt feed my people Israel, and thou shalt be a captain over Israel.

110.   Thus, whether a family by degrees grew up into a commonwealth, and the fatherly authority being continued on to the

elder son, every one in his turn growing up under it, tacitly submitted to it, and the easiness and equality of it not offending any one, every one acquiesced, till time seemed to have confirmed it, and settled a right of succession by prescription: or whether several families, or the descendants of several families, whom chance, neighbourhood, or business brought together, uniting into society, the need of a general, whose conduct might defend them against their enemies in war, and the great confidence the innocence and sincerity of that poor but virtuous age, (such as are almost all those which begin governments, that ever come to last in the world) gave men one of another, made the first beginners of commonwealths generally put the rule into one man's hand, without any other express limitation or restraint, but what the nature of the thing, and the end of government required: which ever of those it was that at first put the rule into the hands of a single person, certain it is no body was entrusted with it but for the public good and safety, and to those ends, in the infancies of commonwealths, those who had it commonly used it. And unless they had done so, young societies could not have subsisted; without such nursing fathers tender and careful of the public weal, all governments would have sunk under the weakness and infirmities of their infancy, and the prince and the people had soon perished together.

111. But though the golden age (before vain ambition, and *amor sceleratus habendi*, evil concupiscence, had corrupted men's minds into a mistake of true power and honour) had more virtue, and consequently better governors, as well as less vicious subjects, and there was then no stretching prerogative on the one side, to oppress the people; nor consequently on the other, any dispute about privilege, to lessen or restrain the power of the magistrate, and so no contest betwixt rulers and people about governors or government: yet, when ambition and luxury in future ages would retain and increase the power, without doing the business for which it was given; and aided by flattery, taught princes to have distinct and separate interests from their people, men found it necessary to examine more carefully the original and rights of government; and to find out ways to restrain the exorbitances, and prevent the abuses of that power, which they having entrusted in another's hands only for their own good, they found was made use of to hurt them.

112. Thus we may see how probable it is, that people that were naturally free, and by their own consent either submitted to the government of their father, or united together out of different families to make a government, should generally put the rule into one man's hands, and choose to be under the conduct of a single person, without so much as by express conditions limiting or regulating his power, which they thought safe enough in his honesty and prudence; though they never dreamed of monarchy being *Iure Divino*, [by divine right] which we never heard of among mankind, till it was revealed to us by the divinity of this last age; nor ever allowed paternal power to have a right to dominion, or to be the foundation of all government. And thus much may suffice to show, that as far as we have any light from history, we have reason to conclude, that all peaceful beginnings of government have been laid in the consent of the people. I say peaceful, because I shall have occasion in another place to speak of conquest, which some esteem a way of beginning of governments.

The other objection I find urged against the beginning of polities, in the way I have mentioned, is this, viz.

113. That all men being born under government, some or other, it is impossible any of them should ever be free, and at liberty to unite together, and begin a new one, or ever be able to erect a lawful government.

If this argument be good; I ask, how came so many lawful monarchies into the world? for if any body, upon this supposition, can show me any one man in any age of the world free to begin a lawful monarchy, I will be bound to show him ten other free men at liberty, at the same time to unite and begin a new government under a regal, or any other form; it being demonstration, that if any one, born under the dominion of another, may be so free as to have a right to command others in a new and distinct empire, every one that is born under the dominion of another may be so free too, and may become a ruler, or subject, of a distinct separate government. And so by this their own principle, either all men, however born, are free, or else there is but one lawful prince, one lawful government in the world. And then they have nothing to do, but barely to show us which that is; which when they have done, I doubt not but all mankind will easily agree to pay obedience to him.

114. Though it be a sufficient answer to their objection, to show that it involves them in the same difficulties that it doth those they use it against; yet I shall endeavour to discover the weakness of this argument a little farther. All men, say they, are born under government, and therefore they cannot be at liberty to begin a new one. Every one is born a subject to his father, or his prince, and is therefore under the perpetual tie of subjection and allegiance. It is plain mankind never owned nor considered any such natural subjection that they were born in, to one or to the other that tied them, without their own consents, to a subjection to them and their heirs.

115. For there are no examples so frequent in history, both sacred and profane, as those of men withdrawing themselves, and their obedience, from the jurisdiction they were born under, and the family or community they were bred up in, and setting up new governments in other places; from whence sprang all that number of petty commonwealths in the beginning of ages, and which always multiplied, as long as there was room enough, till the stronger, or more fortunate, swallowed the weaker; and those great ones again breaking to pieces, dissolved into lesser dominions. All which are so many testimonies against paternal sovereignty, and plainly prove, that it was not the natural right of the father descending to his heirs, that made governments in the beginning, since it was impossible, upon that ground, there should have been so many little kingdoms; all must have been but only one universal monarchy, if men had not been at liberty to separate themselves from their families, and the government, be it what it will, that was set up in it, and go and make distinct commonwealths and other governments, as they thought fit.

116. This has been the practice of the world from its first beginning to this day; nor is it now any more hindrance to the freedom of mankind, that they are born under constituted and ancient polities, that have established laws, and set forms of government, than if they were born in the woods, amongst the unconfined inhabitants, that run loose in them: for those, who would persuade us, that by being born under any government, we are naturally subjects to it, and have no more any title or pretence to the freedom of the state of nature, have no other reason (barring that of paternal power, which we have already answered) to produce for it, but only, because our fathers or progenitors passed away their natural liberty, and thereby bound up

themselves and their posterity to a perpetual subjection to the government, which they themselves submitted to. It is true, that whatever engagements or promises any one has made for himself, he is under the obligation of them, but cannot, by any compact whatsoever, bind his children or posterity: for his son, when a man, being altogether as free as the father, any act of the father can no more give away the liberty of the son, than it can of any body else: he may indeed annex such conditions to the land, he enjoyed as a subject of any commonwealth, as may oblige his son to be of that community, if he will enjoy those possessions which were his father's; because that estate being his father's property, he may dispose, or settle it, as he pleases.

117. And this has generally given the occasion to mistake in this matter; because commonwealths not permitting any part of their dominions to be dismembered, nor to be enjoyed by any but those of their community, the son cannot ordinarily enjoy the possessions of his father, but under the same terms his father did, by becoming a member of the society; whereby he puts himself presently under the government he finds there established, as much as any other subject of that commonwealth. And thus the consent of freemen, born under government, which only makes them members of it, being given separately in their turns, as each comes to be of age, and not in a multitude together; people take no notice of it, and thinking it not done at all, or not necessary, conclude they are naturally subjects as they are men.

118. But, it is plain, governments themselves understand it otherwise; they claim no power over the son, because of that they had over the father; nor look on children as being their subjects, by their fathers being so. If a subject of England have a child, by an English woman in France, whose subject is he? Not the king of England's; for he must have leave to be admitted to the privileges of it: nor the king of France's; for how then has his father a liberty to bring him away, and breed him as he pleases? and who ever was judged as a traitor or deserter, if he left, or warred against a country, for being barely born in it of parents that were aliens there? It is plain then, by the practice of governments themselves, as well as by the law of right reason, that a child is born a subject of no country or government. He is under his father's tuition and authority, till he comes to age of discretion; and

then he is a freeman, at liberty what government he will put himself under, what body politic he will unite himself to: for if an Englishman's son, born in France, be at liberty, and may do so, it is evident there is no tie upon him by his father's being a subject of this kingdom; nor is he bound up by any compact of his ancestors. And why then hath not his son, by the same reason, the same liberty, though he be born anywhere else? Since the power that a father hath naturally over his children, is the same, where-ever they be born, and the ties of natural obligations, are not bounded by the positive limits of kingdoms and commonwealths.

119. Every man being, as has been shown, naturally free, and nothing being able to put him into subjection to any earthly power, but only his own consent; it is to be considered, what shall be understood to be a sufficient declaration of a man's consent, to make him subject to the laws of any government. There is a common distinction of an express and a tacit consent, which will concern our present case. No body doubts but an express consent, of any man entering into any society, makes him a perfect member of that society, a subject of that government. The difficulty is, what ought to be looked upon as a tacit consent, and how far it binds, i.e. how far any one shall be looked on to have consented, and thereby submitted to any government, where he has made no expressions of it at all. And to this I say, that every man, that hath any possessions, or enjoyment, of any part of the dominions of any government, doth thereby give his tacit consent, and is as far forth obliged to obedience to the laws of that government, during such enjoyment, as any one under it; whether this his possession be of land, to him and his heirs for ever, or a lodging only for a week; or whether it be barely travelling freely on the highway; and in effect, it reaches as far as the very being of any one within the territories of that government.

120. To understand this the better, it is fit to consider, that every man, when he at first incorporates himself into any commonwealth, he, by his uniting himself thereunto, annexed also, and submits to the community, those possessions, which he has, or shall acquire, that do not already belong to any other government: for it would be a direct contradiction, for any one to enter into society with others for the securing and regulating of property; and yet to suppose his land, whose property is to be regulated by the laws of the society, should be

exempt from the jurisdiction of that government, to which he himself, the proprietor of the land, is a subject.   By the same act therefore, whereby any one unites his person, which was before free, to any commonwealth, by the same he unites his possessions, which were before free, to it also; and they become, both of them, person and possession, subject to the government and dominion of that commonwealth, as long as it hath a being. Whoever therefore, from thenceforth, by inheritance, purchase, permission, or otherwise, enjoys any part of the land, so annexed to, and under the government of that commonwealth, must take it with the condition it is under; that is, of submitting to the government of the commonwealth, under whose jurisdiction it is, as far forth as any subject of it.

121. But since the government has a direct jurisdiction only over the land, and reaches the possessor of it, (before he has actually incorporated himself in the society) only as he dwells upon, and enjoys that; the obligation any one is under, by virtue of such enjoyment, to submit to the government, begins and ends with the enjoyment; so that whenever the owner, who has given nothing but such a tacit consent to the government, will, by donation, sale, or otherwise, quit the said possession, he is at liberty to go and incorporate himself into any other commonwealth; or to agree with others to begin a new one, *in vacuis locis*, [in empty places] in any part of the world, they can find free and unpossessed: whereas he, that has once, by actual agreement, and any express declaration, given his consent to be of any commonwealth, is perpetually and indispensably obliged to be, and remain unalterably a subject to it, and can never be again in the liberty of the state of nature; unless, by any calamity, the government he was under comes to be dissolved; or else by some public act cuts him off from being any longer a member of it.

122. But submitting to the laws of any country, living quietly, and enjoying privileges and protection under them, makes not a man a member of that society: this is only a local protection and homage due to and from all those, who, not being in a state of war, come within the territories belonging to any government, to all parts whereof the force of its laws extends. But this no more makes a man a member of that society, a perpetual subject of that commonwealth, than it would make a man a subject to another, in whose family he found it convenient to abide for some time; though, whilst he continued in it, he were obliged

to comply with the laws, and submit to the government he found there. And thus we see, that foreigners, by living all their lives under another government, and enjoying the privileges and protection of it, though they are bound, even in conscience, to submit to its administration, as far forth as any denison; yet do not thereby come to be subjects or members of that commonwealth. Nothing can make any man so, but his actually entering into it by positive engagement, and express promise and compact. This is that, which I think, concerning the beginning of political societies, and that consent which makes any one a member of any commonwealth.

Of the Ends of Political Society and Government.

123. If man in the state of nature be so free, as has been said; if he be absolute lord of his own person and possessions, equal to the greatest, and subject to no body, why will he part with his freedom? why will he give up this empire, and subject himself to the dominion and control of any other power? To which it is obvious to answer, that though in the state of nature he hath such a right, yet the enjoyment of it is very uncertain, and constantly exposed to the invasion of others: for all being kings as much as he, every man his equal, and the greater part no strict observers of equity and justice, the enjoyment of the property he has in this state is very unsafe, very insecure. This makes him willing to quit a condition, which, however free, is full of fears and continual dangers: and it is not without reason, that he seeks out, and is willing to join in society with others, who are already united, or have a mind to unite, for the mutual preservation of their lives, liberties and estates, which I call by the general name, property.

124. The great and chief end, therefore, of men's uniting into commonwealths, and putting themselves under government, is the preservation of their property. To which in the state of nature there are many things wanting.

First, There wants an established, settled, known law, received and allowed by common consent to be the standard of right and wrong, and the common measure to decide all controversies between them: for though the law of nature be plain and intelligible to all rational creatures; yet men being biased by their interest, as well as ignorant for want of study of it, are not apt to allow of it as a law binding to them in the application of it to their particular cases.

125. Secondly, In the state of nature there wants a known and indifferent judge, with authority to determine all differences according to the established law: for every one in that state being both judge and executioner of the law of nature, men being partial to themselves, passion and revenge is very apt to carry them too far, and with too much heat, in their own cases; as well as negligence, and unconcernedness, to make them too remiss in other men's.

126. Thirdly, In the state of nature there often wants power to back and support the sentence when right, and to give it due execution, They who by any injustice offended, will seldom fail, where they are able, by force to make good their injustice; such resistance many times makes the punishment dangerous, and frequently destructive, to those who attempt it.

127. Thus mankind, notwithstanding all the privileges of the state of nature, being but in an ill condition, while they remain in it, are quickly driven into society. Hence it comes to pass, that we seldom find any number of men live any time together in this state. The inconveniencies that they are therein exposed to, by the irregular and uncertain exercise of the power every man has of punishing the transgressions of others, make them take sanctuary under the established laws of government, and therein seek the preservation of their property. It is this makes them so willingly give up every one his single power of punishing, to be exercised by such alone, as shall be appointed to it amongst them; and by such rules as the community, or those authorised by them to that purpose, shall agree on. And in this we have the original right and rise of both the legislative and executive power, as well as of the governments and societies themselves.

128. For in the state of nature, to omit the liberty he has of innocent delights, a man has two powers.

The first is to do whatsoever he thinks fit for the preservation of himself, and others within the permission of the law of nature: by which law, common to them all, he and all the rest of mankind are one community, make up one society, distinct from all other creatures. And were it not for the corruption and viciousness of degenerate men, there would be no need of any other; no necessity that men should separate from this great and natural community, and by positive agreements combine into smaller and divided associations.

The other power a man has in the state of nature, is the power to punish the crimes committed against that law. Both these he gives up, when he joins in a private, if I may so call it, or particular politic society, and incorporates into any commonwealth, separate from the rest of mankind.

129. The first power, viz. of doing whatsoever he thought for the preservation of himself, and the rest of mankind, he gives up to be regulated by laws made by the society, so far forth as the preservation of himself, and the rest of that society shall require; which laws of the society in many things confine the liberty he had by the law of nature.

130. Secondly, The power of punishing he wholly gives up, and engages his natural force, (which he might before employ in the execution of the law of nature, by his own single authority, as he thought fit) to assist the executive power of the society, as the law thereof shall require: for being now in a new state, wherein he is to enjoy many conveniencies, from the labour, assistance, and society of others in the same community, as well as protection from its whole strength; he is to part also with as much of his natural liberty, in providing for himself, as the good, prosperity, and safety of the society shall require; which is not only necessary, but just, since the other members of the society do the like.

131. But though men, when they enter into society, give up the equality, liberty, and executive power they had in the state of nature, into the hands of the society, to be so far disposed of by the legislative, as the good of the society shall require; yet it being only with an intention in every one the better to preserve himself, his liberty and property; (for no rational creature can be supposed to change his condition with an intention to be worse) the power of the society, or legislative constituted by them, can never be supposed to extend farther, than the common good; but is obliged to secure every one's property, by providing against those three defects above mentioned, that made the state of nature so unsafe and uneasy. And so whoever has the legislative or supreme power of any commonwealth, is bound to govern by established standing laws, promulgated and known to the people, and not by extemporary decrees; by indifferent and upright judges, who are to decide controversies by those laws; and to employ the force of the community at home, only in the execution of such laws, or abroad to prevent or redress foreign injuries, and secure the

community from inroads and invasion. And all this to be directed to no other end, but the peace, safety, and public good of the people.

Of the Forms of a Commonwealth.

132. The majority having, as has been shown, upon men's first uniting into society, the whole power of the community naturally in them, may employ all that power in making laws for the community from time to time, and executing those laws by officers of their own appointing; and then the form of the government is a perfect democracy: or else may put the power of making laws into the hands of a few select men, and their heirs or successors; and then it is an oligarchy: or else into the hands of one man, and then it is a monarchy: if to him and his heirs, it is an hereditary monarchy: if to him only for life, but upon his death the power only of nominating a successor to return to them; an elective monarchy. And so accordingly of these the community may make compounded and mixed forms of government, as they think good. And if the legislative power be at first given by the majority to one or more persons only for their lives, or any limited time, and then the supreme power to revert to them again; when it is so reverted, the community may dispose of it again anew into what hands they please, and so constitute a new form of government: for the form of government depending upon the placing the supreme power, which is the legislative, it being impossible to conceive that an inferior power should prescribe to a superior, or any but the supreme make laws, according as the power of making laws is placed, such is the form of the commonwealth.

133. By commonwealth, I must be understood all along to mean, not a democracy, or any form of government, but any independent community, which the Latins signified by the word civitas, to which the word which best answers in our language, is commonwealth, and most properly expresses such a society of men, which community or city in English does not; for there may be subordinate communities in a government; and city amongst us has a quite different notion from commonwealth: and therefore, to avoid ambiguity, I crave leave to use the word commonwealth in that sense, in which I find it used by king James the first; and I take it to be its genuine signification; which if any body dislike, I consent with him to change it for a better.

Of the Extent of the Legislative Power.

134. The great end of men's entering into society, being the enjoyment of their properties in peace and safety, and the great instrument and means of that being the laws established in that society; the first and fundamental positive law of all commonwealths is the establishing of the legislative power; as the first and fundamental natural law, which is to govern even the legislative itself, is the preservation of the society, and (as far as will consist with the public good) of every person in it. This legislative is not only the supreme power of the commonwealth, but sacred and unalterable in the hands where the community have once placed it; nor can any edict of any body else, in what form soever conceived, or by what power soever backed, have the force and obligation of a law, which has not its sanction from that legislative which the public has chosen and appointed: for without this the law could not have that, which is absolutely necessary to its being a law, the consent of the society, over whom no body can have a power to make laws, but by their own consent, and by authority received from them; and therefore all the obedience, which by the most solemn ties any one can be obliged to pay, ultimately terminates in this supreme power, and is directed by those laws which it enacts: nor can any oaths to any foreign power whatsoever, or any domestic subordinate power, discharge any member of the society from his obedience to the legislative, acting pursuant to their trust; nor oblige him to any obedience contrary to the laws so enacted, or farther than they do allow; it being ridiculous to imagine one can be tied ultimately to obey any power in the society, which is not the supreme.

135. Though the legislative, whether placed in one or more, whether it be always in being, or only by intervals, though it be the supreme power in every commonwealth; yet,

First, It is not, nor can possibly be absolutely arbitrary over the lives and fortunes of the people: for it being but the joint power of every member of the society given up to that person, or assembly, which is legislator; it can be no more than those persons had in a state of nature before they entered into society, and gave up to the community: for no body can transfer to another more power than he has in himself; and no body has an absolute arbitrary power over himself, or over any other, to destroy his own life, or take away the life or property of another. A man, as has been proved, cannot subject himself to the arbitrary power of another; and having in the state of nature no arbitrary power over the life, liberty, or possession of another, but only so much as the law of nature gave him for the preservation of himself, and the rest of mankind; this is all he doth, or can give up to the commonwealth, and by it to the legislative power, so that the legislative can have no more than this. Their power, in the utmost bounds of it, is limited to the public good of the society. It is a power, that hath no other end but preservation, and therefore can never have a right to destroy, enslave, or designedly to impoverish the subjects. The obligations of the law of nature cease not in society, but only in many cases are drawn closer, and have by human laws known penalties annexed to them, to enforce their observation. Thus the law of nature stands as an eternal rule to all men, legislators as well as others. The rules that they make for other men's actions, must, as well as their own and other men's actions, be conformable to the law of nature, i.e. to the will of God, of which that is a declaration, and the fundamental law of nature being the preservation of mankind, no human sanction can be good, or valid against it.

136. Secondly, The legislative, or supreme authority, cannot assume to its self a power to rule by extemporary arbitrary decrees, but is bound to dispense justice, and decide the rights of the subject by promulgated standing laws, and known authorised judges: for the law of nature being unwritten, and so nowhere to be found but in the minds of men, they who through passion or interest shall miscite, or misapply it, cannot so easily be convinced of their mistake where there is no established judge: and so it serves not, as it ought, to determine the rights, and fence the properties of those that live under it, especially where every one is judge, interpreter, and executioner of it too, and that in his own case: and he that has right on his side, having ordinarily but his own single strength, hath not force enough to defend himself from injuries, or to punish delinquents. To avoid these inconveniences, which disorder men's properties in the state of nature, men unite into societies, that they may have the united strength of the whole society to secure and defend their properties, and may have standing rules to bound it, by which every one may know what is his. To this end it is that men give up all their natural power to the society which they enter into, and the community put the legislative power

into such hands as they think fit, with this trust, that they shall be governed by declared laws, or else their peace, quiet, and property will still be at the same uncertainty, as it was in the state of nature.

137. Absolute arbitrary power, or governing without settled standing laws, can neither of them consist with the ends of society and government, which men would not quit the freedom of the state of nature for, and tie themselves up under, were it not to preserve their lives, liberties and fortunes, and by stated rules of right and property to secure their peace and quiet. It cannot be supposed that they should intend, had they a power so to do, to give to any one, or more, an absolute arbitrary power over their persons and estates, and put a force into the magistrate's hand to execute his unlimited will arbitrarily upon them. This were to put themselves into a worse condition than the state of nature, wherein they had a liberty to defend their right against the injuries of others, and were upon equal terms of force to maintain it, whether invaded by a single man, or many in combination. Whereas by supposing they have given up themselves to the absolute arbitrary power and will of a legislator, they have disarmed themselves, and armed him, to make a prey of them when he pleases; he being in a much worse condition, who is exposed to the arbitrary power of one man, who has the command of 100,000, than he that is exposed to the arbitrary power of 100,000 single men; no body being secure, that his will, who has such a command, is better than that of other men, though his force be 100,000 times stronger. And therefore, whatever form the commonwealth is under, the ruling power ought to govern by declared and received laws, and not by extemporary dictates and undetermined resolutions: for then mankind will be in a far worse condition than in the state of nature, if they shall have armed one, or a few men with the joint power of a multitude, to force them to obey at pleasure the exorbitant and unlimited decrees of their sudden thoughts, or unrestrained, and till that moment unknown wills, without having any measures set down which may guide and justify their actions: for all the power the government has, being only for the good of the society, as it ought not to be arbitrary and at pleasure, so it ought to be exercised by established and promulgated laws; that both the people may know their duty, and be safe and secure within the limits of the law; and the rulers too kept within their bounds, and not be tempted, by the power they have in their hands, to employ it to such purposes,

and by such measures, as they would not have known, and own not willingly.

138. Thirdly, The supreme power cannot take from any man any part of his property without his own consent: for the preservation of property being the end of government, and that for which men enter into society, it necessarily supposes and requires, that the people should have property, without which they must be supposed to lose that, by entering into society, which was the end for which they entered into it; too gross an absurdity for any man to own. Men therefore in society having property, they have such a right to the goods, which by the law of the community are theirs, that no body hath a right to take their substance or any part of it from them, without their own consent: without this they have no property at all; for I have truly no property in that, which another can by right take from me, when he pleases, against my consent. Hence it is a mistake to think, that the supreme or legislative power of any commonwealth, can do what it will, and dispose of the estates of the subject arbitrarily, or take any part of them at pleasure. This is not much to be feared in governments where the legislative consists, wholly or in part, in assemblies which are variable, whose members, upon the dissolution of the assembly, are subjects under the common laws of their country, equally with the rest. But in governments, where the legislative is in one lasting assembly always in being, or in one man, as in absolute monarchies, there is danger still, that they will think themselves to have a distinct interest from the rest of the community; and so will be apt to increase their own riches and power, by taking what they think fit from the people: for a man's property is not at all secure, though there be good and equitable laws to set the bounds of it between him and his fellow subjects, if he who commands those subjects have power to take from any private man, what part he pleases of his property, and use and dispose of it as he thinks good.

139. But government, into whatsoever hands it is put, being, as I have before shown, entrusted with this condition, and for this end, that men might have and secure their properties; the prince, or senate, however it may have power to make laws, for the regulating of property between the subjects one amongst another, yet can never have a power to take to themselves the whole, or any part of the subjects property, without their own consent: for this would be in effect to

leave them no property at all. And to let us see, that even absolute power, where it is necessary, is not arbitrary by being absolute, but is still limited by that reason, and confined to those ends, which required it in some cases to be absolute, we need look no farther than the common practice of martial discipline: for the preservation of the army, and in it of the whole commonwealth, requires an absolute obedience to the command of every superior officer, and it is justly death to disobey or dispute the most dangerous or unreasonable of them; but yet we see, that neither the sergeant, that could command a soldier to march up to the mouth of a cannon, or stand in a breach, where he is almost sure to perish, can command that soldier to give him one penny of his money; nor the general, that can condemn him to death for deserting his post, or for not obeying the most desperate orders, can yet, with all his absolute power of life and death, dispose of one farthing of that soldier's estate, or seize one jot of his goods; whom yet he can command any thing, and hang for the least disobedience; because such a blind obedience is necessary to that end, for which the commander has his power, viz. the preservation of the rest; but the disposing of his goods has nothing to do with it.

140. It is true, governments cannot be supported without great charge, and it is fit every one who enjoys his share of the protection, should pay out of his estate his proportion for the maintenance of it. But still it must be with his own consent, i.e. the consent of the majority, giving it either by themselves, or their representatives chosen by them: for if any one shall claim a power to lay and levy taxes on the people, by his own authority, and without such consent of the people, he thereby invades the fundamental law of property, and subverts the end of government: for what property have I in that, which another may by right take, when he pleases, to himself?

141. Fourthly, The legislative cannot transfer the power of making laws to any other hands: for it being but a delegated power from the people, they who have it cannot pass it over to others. The people alone can appoint the form of the commonwealth, which is by constituting the legislative, and appointing in whose hands that shall be. And when the people have said, We will submit to rules, and be governed by laws made by such men, and in such forms, no body else can say other men shall make laws for them; nor can the people be bound by any laws, but such as are enacted by those whom they have

chosen, and authorised to make laws for them. The power of the legislative, being derived from the people by a positive voluntary grant and institution, can be no other than what that positive grant conveyed, which being only to make laws, and not to make legislators, the legislative can have no power to transfer their authority of making laws, and place it in other hands.

142. These are the bounds which the trust, that is put in them by the society, and the law of God and nature, have set to the legislative power of every commonwealth, in all forms of government.

First, They are to govern by promulgated established laws, not to be varied in particular cases, but to have one rule for rich and poor, for the favourite at court, and the country man at plough.

Secondly, These laws also ought to be designed for no other end ultimately, but the good of the people.

Thirdly, They must not raise taxes on the property of the people, without the consent of the people, given by themselves, or their deputies. And this properly concerns only such governments where the legislative is always in being, or at least where the people have not reserved any part of the legislative to deputies, to be from time to time chosen by themselves.

Fourthly, The legislative neither must nor can transfer the power of making laws to any body else, or place it anywhere, but where the people have.

Of the Legislative, Executive, and Federative Power of the Commonwealth.

143. The legislative power is that, which has a right to direct how the force of the commonwealth shall be employed for preserving the community and the members of it. But because those laws which are constantly to be executed, and whose force is always to continue, may be made in a little time; therefore there is no need, that the legislative should be always in being, not having always business to do. And because it may be too great a temptation to human frailty, apt to grasp at power, for the same persons, who have the power of making laws, to have also in their hands the power to execute them, whereby they may exempt themselves from obedience to the laws they make, and suit the law, both in its making, and execution, to their own private advantage, and thereby come to have a distinct interest from the rest of the community, contrary to the end of society and government: therefore

in well ordered commonwealths, where the good of the whole is so considered, as it ought, the legislative power is put into the hands of divers persons, who duly assembled, have by themselves, or jointly with others, a power to make laws, which when they have done, being separated again, they are themselves subject to the laws they have made; which is a new and near tie upon them, to take care, that they make them for the public good.

144. But because the laws, that are at once, and in a short time made, have a constant and lasting force, and need a perpetual execution, or an attendance thereunto; therefore it is necessary there should be a power always in being, which should see to the execution of the laws that are made, and remain in force. And thus the legislative and executive power come often to be separated.

145. There is another power in every commonwealth, which one may call natural, because it is that which answers to the power every man naturally had before he entered into society: for though in a commonwealth the members of it are distinct persons still in reference to one another, and as such as governed by the laws of the society; yet in reference to the rest of mankind, they make one body, which is, as every member of it before was, still in the state of nature with the rest of mankind. Hence it is, that the controversies that happen between any man of the society with those that are out of it, are managed by the public; and an injury done to a member of their body, engages the whole in the reparation of it. So that under this consideration, the whole community is one body in the state of nature, in respect of all other states or persons out of its community.

146. This therefore contains the power of war and peace, leagues and alliances, and all the transactions, with all persons and communities without the commonwealth, and may be called federative, if any one pleases. So the thing be understood, I am indifferent as to the name.

147. These two powers, executive and federative, though they be really distinct in themselves, yet one comprehending the execution of the municipal laws of the society within its self, upon all that are parts of it; the other the management of the security and interest of the public without, with all those that it may receive benefit or damage from, yet they are always almost united. And though this federative power in the well or ill management of it be of great moment to the

commonwealth, yet it is much less capable to be directed by antecedent, standing, positive laws, than the executive; and so must necessarily be left to the prudence and wisdom of those, whose hands it is in, to be managed for the public good: for the laws that concern subjects one amongst another, being to direct their actions, may well enough precede them. But what is to be done in reference to foreigners, depending much upon their actions, and the variation of designs and interests, must be left in great part to the prudence of those, who have this power committed to them, to be managed by the best of their skill, for the advantage of the commonwealth.

148. Though, as I said, the executive and federative power of every community be really distinct in themselves, yet they are hardly to be separated, and placed at the same time, in the hands of distinct persons: for both of them requiring the force of the society for their exercise, it is almost impracticable to place the force of the commonwealth in distinct, and not subordinate hands; or that the executive and federative power should be placed in persons, that might act separately, whereby the force of the public would be under different commands: which would be apt some time or other to cause disorder and ruin.

Of the Subordination of the Powers of the Commonwealth.

149. Though in a constituted commonwealth, standing upon its own basis, and acting according to its own nature, that is, acting for the preservation of the community, there can be but one supreme power, which is the legislative, to which all the rest are and must be subordinate, yet the legislative being only a fiduciary power to act for certain ends, there remains still in the people a supreme power to remove or alter the legislative, when they find the legislative act contrary to the trust reposed in them: for all power given with trust for the attaining an end, being limited by that end, whenever that end is manifestly neglected, or opposed, the trust must necessarily be forfeited, and the power devolve into the hands of those that gave it, who may place it anew where they shall think best for their safety and security. And thus the community perpetually retains a supreme power of saving themselves from the attempts and designs of any body, even of their legislators, whenever they shall be so foolish, or so wicked, as to lay and carry on designs against the liberties and properties of the subject: for no man or society of men, having a power

to deliver up their preservation, or consequently the means of it, to the absolute will and arbitrary dominion of another; when ever any one shall go about to bring them into such a slavish condition, they will always have a right to preserve, what they have not a power to part with; and to rid themselves of those, who invade this fundamental, sacred, and unalterable law of self-preservation, for which they entered into society. And thus the community may be said in this respect to be always the supreme power, but not as considered under any form of government, because this power of the people can never take place till the government be dissolved.

150. In all cases, whilst the government subsists, the legislative is the supreme power: for what can give laws to another, must needs be superior to him; and since the legislative is no otherwise legislative of the society, but by the right it has to make laws for all the parts, and for every member of the society, prescribing rules to their actions, and giving power of execution, where they are transgressed, the legislative must needs be the supreme, and all other powers, in any members or parts of the society, derived from and subordinate to it.

151. In some commonwealths, where the legislative is not always in being, and the executive is vested in a single person, who has also a share in the legislative; there that single person in a very tolerable sense may also be called supreme: not that he has in himself all the supreme power, which is that of law-making; but because he has in him the supreme execution, from whom all inferior magistrates derive all their several subordinate powers, or at least the greatest part of them: having also no legislative superior to him, there being no law to be made without his consent, which cannot be expected should ever subject him to the other part of the legislative, he is properly enough in this sense supreme. But yet it is to be observed, that though oaths of allegiance and fealty are taken to him, it is not to him as supreme legislator, but as supreme executor of the law, made by a joint power of him with others; allegiance being nothing but an obedience according to law, which when he violates, he has no right to obedience, nor can claim it otherwise than as the public person vested with the power of the law, and so is to be considered as the image, phantom, or representative of the commonwealth, acted by the will of the society, declared in its laws; and thus he has no will, no power, but that of the law. But when he quits this representation, this public will,

and acts by his own private will, he degrades himself, and is but a single private person without power, and without will, that has any right to obedience; the members owing no obedience but to the public will of the society.

152. The executive power, placed anywhere but in a person that has also a share in the legislative, is visibly subordinate and accountable to it, and may be at pleasure changed and displaced; so that it is not the supreme executive power, that is exempt from subordination, but the supreme executive power vested in one, who having a share in the legislative, has no distinct superior legislative to be subordinate and accountable to, farther than he himself shall join and consent; so that he is no more subordinate than he himself shall think fit, which one may certainly conclude will be but very little. Of other ministerial and subordinate powers in a commonwealth, we need not speak, they being so multiplied with infinite variety, in the different customs and constitutions of distinct commonwealths, that it is impossible to give a particular account of them all. Only thus much, which is necessary to our present purpose, we may take notice of concerning them, that they have no manner of authority, any of them, beyond what is by positive grant and commission delegated to them, and are all of them accountable to some other power in the commonwealth.

153. It is not necessary, no, nor so much as convenient, that the legislative should be always in being; but absolutely necessary that the executive power should, because there is not always need of new laws to be made, but always need of execution of the laws that are made. When the legislative hath put the execution of the laws, they make, into other hands, they have a power still to resume it out of those hands, when they find cause, and to punish for any maladministration against the laws. The same holds also in regard of the federative power, that and the executive being both ministerial and subordinate to the legislative, which, as has been shown, in a constituted commonwealth is the supreme. The legislative also in this case being supposed to consist of several persons, (for if it be a single person, it cannot but be always in being, and so will, as supreme, naturally have the supreme executive power, together with the legislative) may assemble, and exercise their legislature, at the times that either their original constitution, or their own adjournment, appoints, or when they

please; if neither of these hath appointed any time, or there be no other way prescribed to convoke them: for the supreme power being placed in them by the people, it is always in them, and they may exercise it when they please, unless by their original constitution they are limited to certain seasons, or by an act of their supreme power they have adjourned to a certain time; and when that time comes, they have a right to assemble and act again.

154. If the legislative, or any part of it, be made up of representatives chosen for that time by the people, which afterwards return into the ordinary state of subjects, and have no share in the legislature but upon a new choice, this power of choosing must also be exercised by the people, either at certain appointed seasons, or else when they are summoned to it; and in this latter case the power of convoking the legislative is ordinarily placed in the executive, and has one of these two limitations in respect of time: that either the original constitution requires their assembling and acting at certain intervals, and then the executive power does nothing but ministerially issue directions for their electing and assembling, according to due forms; or else it is left to his prudence to call them by new elections, when the occasions or exigencies of the public require the amendment of old, or making of new laws, or the redress or prevention of any inconveniencies, that lie on, or threaten the people.

155. It may be demanded here, What if the executive power, being possessed of the force of the commonwealth, shall make use of that force to hinder the meeting and acting of the legislative, when the original constitution, or the public exigencies require it? I say, using force upon the people without authority, and contrary to the trust put in him that does so, is a state of war with the people, who have a right to reinstate their legislative in the exercise of their power: for having erected a legislative, with an intent they should exercise the power of making laws, either at certain set times, or when there is need of it, when they are hindered by any force from what is so necessary to the society, and wherein the safety and preservation of the people consists, the people have a right to remove it by force. In all states and conditions, the true remedy of force without authority, is to oppose force to it. The use of force without authority, always puts him that uses it into a state of war, as the aggressor, and renders him liable to be treated accordingly.

156. The power of assembling and dismissing the legislative, placed in the executive, gives not the executive a superiority over it, but is a fiduciary trust placed in him, for the safety of the people, in a case where the uncertainty and variableness of human affairs could not bear a steady fixed rule: for it not being possible, that the first framers of the government should, by any foresight, be so much masters of future events, as to be able to prefix so just periods of return and duration to the assemblies of the legislative, in all times to come, that might exactly answer all the exigencies of the commonwealth; the best remedy could be found for this defect, was to trust this to the prudence of one who was always to be present, and whose business it was to watch over the public good. Constant frequent meetings of the legislative, and long continuations of their assemblies, without necessary occasion, could not but be burdensome to the people, and must necessarily in time produce more dangerous inconveniencies, and yet the quick turn of affairs might be sometimes such as to need their present help: any delay of their convening might endanger the public; and sometimes too their business might be so great, that the limited time of their sitting might be too short for their work, and rob the public of that benefit which could be had only from their mature deliberation. What then could be done in this case to prevent the community from being exposed some time or other to eminent hazard, on one side or the other, by fixed intervals and periods, set to the meeting and acting of the legislative, but to entrust it to the prudence of some, who being present, and acquainted with the state of public affairs, might make use of this prerogative for the public good? and where else could this be so well placed as in his hands, who was entrusted with the execution of the laws for the same end? Thus supposing the regulation of times for the assembling and sitting of the legislative, not settled by the original constitution, it naturally fell into the hands of the executive, not as an arbitrary power depending on his good pleasure, but with this trust always to have it exercised only for the public weal, as the occurrences of times and change of affairs might require. Whether settled periods of their convening, or a liberty left to the prince for convoking the legislative, or perhaps a mixture of both, hath the least inconvenience attending it, it is not my business here to inquire, but only to show, that though the executive power may

have the prerogative of convoking and dissolving such conventions of the legislative, yet it is not thereby superior to it.

157. Things of this world are in so constant a flux, that nothing remains long in the same state. Thus people, riches, trade, power, change their stations, flourishing mighty cities come to ruin, and prove in times neglected desolate corners, whilst other unfrequented places grow into populous countries, filled with wealth and inhabitants. But things not always changing equally, and private interest often keeping up customs and privileges, when the reasons of them are ceased, it often comes to pass, that in governments, where part of the legislative consists of representatives chosen by the people, that in tract of time this representation becomes very unequal and disproportionate to the reasons it was at first established upon. To what gross absurdities the following of custom, when reason has left it, may lead, we may be satisfied, when we see the bare name of a town, of which there remains not so much as the ruins, where scarce so much housing as a sheepcote, or more inhabitants than a shepherd is to be found, sends as many representatives to the grand assembly of law-makers, as a whole county numerous in people, and powerful in riches. This strangers stand amazed at, and every one must confess needs a remedy; though most think it hard to find one, because the constitution of the legislative being the original and supreme act of the society, antecedent to all positive laws in it, and depending wholly on the people, no inferior power can alter it. And therefore the people, when the legislative is once constituted, having, in such a government as we have been speaking of, no power to act as long as the government stands; this inconvenience is thought incapable of a remedy.

158. *Salus populi suprema lex,* [The safety of the people is the supreme law.] is certainly so just and fundamental a rule, that he, who sincerely follows it, cannot dangerously err. If therefore the executive, who has the power of convoking the legislative, observing rather the true proportion, than fashion of representation, regulates, not by old custom, but true reason, the number of members, in all places that have a right to be distinctly represented, which no part of the people however incorporated can pretend to, but in proportion to the assistance which it affords to the public, it cannot be judged to have set up a new legislative, but to have restored the old and true one, and to have rectified the disorders which succession of time had insensibly,

as well as inevitably introduced: For it being the interest as well as intention of the people, to have a fair and equal representative; whoever brings it nearest to that, is an undoubted friend to, and establisher of the government, and cannot miss the consent and approbation of the community; prerogative being nothing but a power, in the hands of the prince, to provide for the public good, in such cases, which depending upon unforeseen and uncertain occurrences, certain and unalterable laws could not safely direct; whatsoever shall be done manifestly for the good of the people, and the establishing the government upon its true foundations, is, and always will be, just prerogative, The power of erecting new corporations, and therewith new representatives, carries with it a supposition, that in time the measures of representation might vary, and those places have a just right to be represented which before had none; and by the same reason, those cease to have a right, and be too inconsiderable for such a privilege, which before had it. It is not a change from the present state, which perhaps corruption or decay has introduced, that makes an inroad upon the government, but the tendency of it to injure or oppress the people, and to set up one part or party, with a distinction from, and an unequal subjection of the rest. Whatsoever cannot but be acknowledged to be of advantage to the society, and people in general, upon just and lasting measures, will always, when done, justify itself; and whenever the people shall choose their representatives upon just and undeniably equal measures, suitable to the original frame of the government, it cannot be doubted to be the will and act of the society, whoever permitted or caused them so to do.

Of Tyranny.

199. As usurpation is the exercise of power, which another hath a right to; so tyranny is the exercise of power beyond right, which no body can have a right to. And this is making use of the power any one has in his hands, not for the good of those who are under it, but for his own private separate advantage. When the governor, however entitled, makes not the law, but his will, the rule; and his commands and actions are not directed to the preservation of the properties of his people, but the satisfaction of his own ambition, revenge, covetousness, or any other irregular passion.

200. If one can doubt this to be truth, or reason, because it comes from the obscure hand of a subject, I hope the authority of a king will

make it pass with him. King James the first, in his speech to the parliament, 1603, tells them thus, "I will ever prefer the weal of the public, and of the whole commonwealth, in making of good laws and constitutions, to any particular and private ends of mine; thinking ever the wealth and weal of the commonwealth to be my greatest weal and worldly felicity; a point wherein a lawful king doth directly differ from a tyrant: for I do acknowledge, that the special and greatest point of difference that is between a rightful king and an usurping tyrant, is this, that whereas the proud and ambitious tyrant doth think his kingdom and people are only ordained for satisfaction of his desires and unreasonable appetites, the righteous and just king doth by the contrary acknowledge himself to be ordained for the procuring of the wealth and property of his people," And again, in his speech to the parliament, 1609, he hath these words, "The king binds himself by a double oath, to the observation of the fundamental laws of his kingdom; tacitly, as by being a king, and so bound to protect as well the people, as the laws of his kingdom; and expressly, by his oath at his coronation, so as every just king, in a settled kingdom, is bound to observe that paction made to his people, by his laws, in framing his government agreeable thereunto, according to that paction which God made with Noah after the deluge. Hereafter, seed-time and harvest, and cold and heat, and summer and winter, and day and night, shall not cease while the earth remaineth. And therefore a king governing in a settled kingdom, leaves to be a king, and degenerates into a tyrant, as soon as he leaves off to rule according to his laws," And a little after, "Therefore all kings that are not tyrants, or perjured, will be glad to bound themselves within the limits of their laws; and they that persuade them the contrary, are vipers, and pests both against them and the commonwealth." Thus that learned king, who well understood the notion of things, makes the difference betwixt a king and a tyrant to consist only in this, that one makes the laws the bounds of his power, and the good of the public, the end of his government; the other makes all give way to his own will and appetite.

201. It is a mistake, to think this fault is proper only to monarchies; other forms of government are liable to it, as well as that: for wherever the power, that is put in any hands for the government of the people, and the preservation of their properties, is applied to other ends, and made use of to impoverish, harass, or subdue them to the

arbitrary and irregular commands of those that have it; there it presently becomes tyranny, whether those that thus use it are one or many. Thus we read of the thirty tyrants at Athens, as well as one at Syracuse; and the intolerable dominion of the Decemviri at Rome was nothing better.

202.   Wherever law ends, tyranny begins, if the law be transgressed to another's harm; and whosoever in authority exceeds the power given him by the law, and makes use of the force he has under his command, to compass that upon the subject, which the law allows not, ceases in that to be a magistrate; and, acting without authority, may be opposed, as any other man, who by force invades the right of another. This is acknowledged in subordinate magistrates. He that hath authority to seize my person in the street, may be opposed as a thief and a robber, if he endeavours to break into my house to execute a writ, notwithstanding that I know he has such a warrant, and such a legal authority, as will empower him to arrest me abroad. And why this should not hold in the highest, as well as in the most inferior magistrate, I would gladly be informed. Is it reasonable, that the eldest brother, because he has the greatest part of his father's estate, should thereby have a right to take away any of his younger brothers portions? or that a rich man, who possessed a whole country, should from thence have a right to seize, when he pleased, the cottage and garden of his poor neighbour? The being rightfully possessed of great power and riches, exceedingly beyond the greatest part of the sons of Adam, is so far from being an excuse, much less a reason, for rapine and oppression, which the damaging another without authority is, that it is a great aggravation of it: for the exceeding the bounds of authority is no more a right in a great, than in a petty officer; no more justifiable in a king than a constable; but is so much the worse in him, in that he has more trust put in him, has already a much greater share than the rest of his brethren, and is supposed, from the advantages of his education, employment, and counsellors, to be more knowing in the measures of right and wrong.

203. May the commands then of a prince be opposed? may he be resisted as often as any one shall find himself aggrieved, and but imagine he has not right done him? This will unhinge and overturn all polities, and, instead of government and order, leave nothing but anarchy and confusion.

204. To this I answer, that force is to be opposed to nothing, but to unjust and unlawful force; whoever makes any opposition in any other case, draws on himself a just condemnation both from God and man; and so no such danger or confusion will follow, as is often suggested: for,

205. First, As, in some countries, the person of the prince by the law is sacred; and so, whatever he commands or does, his person is still free from all question or violence, not liable to force, or any judicial censure or condemnation. But yet opposition may be made to the illegal acts of any inferior officer, or other commissioned by him; unless he will, by actually putting himself into a state of war with his people, dissolve the government, and leave them to that defence which belongs to every one in the state of nature: for of such things who can tell what the end will be? and a neighbour kingdom has shown the world an odd example. In all other cases the sacredness of the person exempts him from all inconveniencies, whereby he is secure, whilst the government stands, from all violence and harm whatsoever; than which there cannot be a wiser constitution: for the harm he can do in his own person not being likely to happen often, nor to extend itself far; nor being able by his single strength to subvert the laws, nor oppress the body of the people, should any prince have so much weakness, and ill nature as to be willing to do it, the inconveniency of some particular mischiefs, that may happen sometimes, when a heady prince comes to the throne, are well recompensed by the peace of the public, and security of the government, in the person of the chief magistrate, thus set out of the reach of danger: it being safer for the body, that some few private men should be sometimes in danger to suffer, than that the head of the republic should be easily, and upon slight occasions, exposed.

206. Secondly, But this privilege, belonging only to the king's person, hinders not, but they may be questioned, opposed, and resisted, who use unjust force, though they pretend a commission from him, which the law authorises not; as is plain in the case of him that has the king's writ to arrest a man, which is a full commission from the king; and yet he that has it cannot break open a man's house to do it, nor execute this command of the king upon certain days, nor in certain places, though this commission have no such exception in it; but they are the limitations of the law, which if any one transgress, the king's

commission excuses him not: for the king's authority being given him only by the law, he cannot empower any one to act against the law, or justify him, by his commission, in so doing; the commission, or command of any magistrate, where he has no authority, being as void and insignificant, as that of any private man; the difference between the one and the other, being that the magistrate has some authority so far, and to such ends, and the private man has none at all: for it is not the commission, but the authority, that gives the right of acting; and against the laws there can be no authority. But, notwithstanding such resistance, the king's person and authority are still both secured, and so no danger to governor or government,

207. Thirdly, Supposing a government wherein the person of the chief magistrate is not thus sacred; yet this doctrine of the lawfulness of resisting all unlawful exercises of his power, will not upon every slight occasion endanger him, or embroil the government: for where the injured party may be relieved, and his damages repaired by appeal to the law, there can be no pretence for force, which is only to be used where a man is intercepted from appealing to the law: for nothing is to be accounted hostile force, but where it leaves not the remedy of such an appeal; and it is such force alone, that puts him that uses it into a state of war, and makes it lawful to resist him. A man with a sword in his hand demands my purse in the high-way, when perhaps I have not twelve pence in my pocket: this man I may lawfully kill. To another I deliver £100 to hold only whilst I alight, which he refuses to restore me, when I am got up again, but draws his sword to defend the possession of it by force, if I endeavour to retake it. The mischief this man does me is a hundred, or possibly a thousand times more than the other perhaps intended me (whom I killed before he really did me any); and yet I might lawfully kill the one, and cannot so much as hurt the other lawfully. The reason whereof is plain; because the one using force, which threatened my life, I could not have time to appeal to the law to secure it: and when it was gone, it was too late to appeal. The law could not restore life to my dead carcass: the loss was irreparable; which to prevent, the law of nature gave me a right to destroy him, who had put himself into a state of war with me, and threatened my destruction. But in the other case, my life not being in danger, I may have the benefit of appealing to the law, and have reparation for my £100 that way.

208. Fourthly, But if the unlawful acts done by the magistrate be maintained (by the power he has got), and the remedy which is due by law, be by the same power obstructed; yet the right of resisting, even in such manifest acts of tyranny, will not suddenly, or on slight occasions, disturb the government: for if it reach no farther than some private men's cases, though they have a right to defend themselves, and to recover by force what by unlawful force is taken from them; yet the right to do so will not easily engage them in a contest, wherein they are sure to perish; it being as impossible for one, or a few oppressed men to disturb the government, where the body of the people do not think themselves concerned in it, as for a raving mad-man, or heady malcontent to overturn a well settled state; the people being as little apt to follow the one, as the other.

209. But if either these illegal acts have extended to the majority of the people; or if the mischief and oppression has lighted only on some few, but in such cases, as the precedent, and consequences seem to threaten all; and they are persuaded in their consciences, that their laws, and with them their estates, liberties, and lives are in danger, and perhaps their religion too; how they will be hindered from resisting illegal force, used against them, I cannot tell.   This is an inconvenience, I confess, that attends all governments whatsoever, when the governors have brought it to this pass, to be generally suspected of their people; the most dangerous state which they can possibly put themselves in.   wherein they are the less to be pitied, because it is so easy to be avoided; it being as impossible for a governor, if he really means the good of his people, and the preservation of them, and their laws together, not to make them see and feel it, as it is for the father of a family, not to let his children see he loves, and takes care of them.

210.   But if all the world shall observe pretences of one kind, and actions of another; arts used to elude the law, and the trust of prerogative (which is an arbitrary power in some things left in the prince's hand to do good, not harm to the people) employed contrary to the end for which it was given: if the people shall find the ministers and subordinate magistrates chosen suitable to such ends, and favoured, or laid by, proportionally as they promote or oppose them: if they see several experiments made of arbitrary power, and that religion underhand favoured, (though publicly proclaimed against) which is

readiest to introduce it; and the operators in it supported, as much as may be; and when that cannot be done, yet approved still, and liked the better: if a long train of actions show the councils all tending that way; how can a man any more hinder himself from being persuaded in his own mind, which way things are going; or from casting about how to save himself, than he could from believing the captain of the ship he was in, was carrying him, and the rest of the company, to Algiers, when he found him always steering that course, though cross winds, leaks in his ship, and want of men and provisions did often force him to turn his course another way for some time, which he steadily returned to again, as soon as the wind, weather, and other circumstances would let him?

THE THEORY OF KNOWLEDGE
No Innate Speculative Principles

1. The way shown how we come by any knowledge, sufficient to prove it not innate. It is an established opinion amongst some men, that there are in the understanding certain innate principles; some primary notions, *koinai ennoiai*, [moral notions common to all mankind], characters, as it were stamped upon the mind of man; which the soul receives in its very first being, and brings into the world with it. It would be sufficient to convince unprejudiced readers of the falseness of this supposition, if I should only show (as I hope I shall in the following parts of this Discourse) how men, barely by the use of their natural faculties, may attain to all the knowledge they have, without the help of any innate impressions; and may arrive at certainty, without any such original notions or principles. For I imagine any one will easily grant that it would be impertinent to suppose the ideas of colours innate in a creature to whom God hath given sight, and a power to receive them by the eyes from external objects: and no less unreasonable would it be to attribute several truths to the impressions of nature, and innate characters, when we may observe in ourselves faculties fit to attain as easy and certain knowledge of them as if they were originally imprinted on the mind.

But because a man is not permitted without censure to follow his own thoughts in the search of truth, when they lead him ever so little out of the common road, I shall set down the reasons that made me doubt of the truth of that opinion, as an excuse for my mistake, if I be in one; which I leave to be considered by those who, with me, dispose themselves to embrace truth wherever they find it.

2. General assent the great argument. There is nothing more commonly taken for granted than that there are certain principles, both speculative and practical, (for they speak of both), universally agreed upon by all mankind: which therefore, they argue, must needs be the constant impressions which the souls of men receive in their first beings, and which they bring into the world with them, as necessarily and really as they do any of their inherent faculties.

3. Universal consent proves nothing innate. This argument, drawn from universal consent, has this misfortune in it, that if it were true in matter of fact, that there were certain truths wherein all mankind agreed, it would not prove them innate, if there can be any

other way shown how men may come to that universal agreement, in the things they do consent in, which I presume may be done.

4. "What is, is," and "It is impossible for the same thing to be and not to be," not universally assented to. But, which is worse, this argument of universal consent, which is made use of to prove innate principles, seems to me a demonstration that there are none such: because there are none to which all mankind give an universal assent. I shall begin with the speculative, and instance in those magnified principles of demonstration, "Whatsoever is, is," and "It is impossible for the same thing to be and not to be"; which, of all others, I think have the most allowed title to innate. These have so settled a reputation of maxims universally received, that it will no doubt be thought strange if any one should seem to question it. But yet I take liberty to say, that these propositions are so far from having an universal assent, that there are a great part of mankind to whom they are not so much as known.

5. Not on the mind naturally imprinted, because not known to children, idiots, &c. For, first, it is evident, that all children and idiots have not the least apprehension or thought of them. And the want of that is enough to destroy that universal assent which must needs be the necessary concomitant of all innate truths: it seeming to me near a contradiction to say, that there are truths imprinted on the soul, which it perceives or understands not: imprinting, if it signify anything, being nothing else but the making certain truths to be perceived. For to imprint anything on the mind without the mind's perceiving it, seems to me hardly intelligible. If therefore children and idiots have souls, have minds, with those impressions upon them, they must unavoidably perceive them, and necessarily know and assent to these truths; which since they do not, it is evident that there are no such impressions. For if they are not notions naturally imprinted, how can they be innate? and if they are notions imprinted, how can they be unknown? To say a notion is imprinted on the mind, and yet at the same time to say, that the mind is ignorant of it, and never yet took notice of it, is to make this impression nothing. No proposition can be said to be in the mind which it never yet knew, which it was never yet conscious of. For if any one may, then, by the same reason, all propositions that are true, and the mind is capable ever of assenting to, may be said to be in the mind, and to be imprinted: since, if any one can be said to be in the

mind, which it never yet knew, it must be only because it is capable of knowing it; and so the mind is of all truths it ever shall know. Nay, thus truths may be imprinted on the mind which it never did, nor ever shall know; for a man may live long, and die at last in ignorance of many truths which his mind was capable of knowing, and that with certainty. So that if the capacity of knowing be the natural impression contended for, all the truths a man ever comes to know will, by this account, be every one of them innate; and this great point will amount to no more, but only to a very improper way of speaking; which, whilst it pretends to assert the contrary, says nothing different from those who deny innate principles. For nobody, I think, ever denied that the mind was capable of knowing several truths. The capacity, they say, is innate; the knowledge acquired. But then to what end such contest for certain innate maxims? If truths can be imprinted on the understanding without being perceived, I can see no difference there can be between any truths the mind is capable of knowing in respect of their original: they must all be innate or all adventitious: in vain shall a man go about to distinguish them. He therefore that talks of innate notions in the understanding, cannot (if he intend thereby any distinct sort of truths) mean such truths to be in the understanding as it never perceived, and is yet wholly ignorant of. For if these words "to be in the understanding" have any propriety, they signify to be understood. So that to be in the understanding, and not to be understood; to be in the mind and never to be perceived, is all one as to say anything is and is not in the mind or understanding. If therefore these two propositions, "Whatsoever is, is," and "It is impossible for the same thing to be and not to be," are by nature imprinted, children cannot be ignorant of them: infants, and all that have souls, must necessarily have them in their understandings, know the truth of them, and assent to it.

6. That men know them when they come to the use of reason, answered. To avoid this, it is usually answered, that all men know and assent to them, when they come to the use of reason; and this is enough to prove them innate. I answer:

7. Doubtful expressions, that have scarce any signification, go for clear reasons to those who, being prepossessed, take not the pains to examine even what they themselves say. For, to apply this answer with any tolerable sense to our present purpose, it must signify one of these two things: either that as soon as men come to the use of reason

these supposed native inscriptions come to be known and observed by them; or else, that the use and exercise of men's reason, assists them in the discovery of these principles, and certainly makes them known to them.

8. If reason discovered them, that would not prove them innate. If they mean, that by the use of reason men may discover these principles, and that this is sufficient to prove them innate; their way of arguing will stand thus, viz. that whatever truths reason can certainly discover to us, and make us firmly assent to, those are all naturally imprinted on the mind; since that universal assent, which is made the mark of them, amounts to no more but this,- that by the use of reason we are capable to come to a certain knowledge of and assent to them; and, by this means, there will be no difference between the maxims of the mathematicians, and theorems they deduce from them: all must be equally allowed innate; they being all discoveries made by the use of reason, and truths that a rational creature may certainty come to know, if he apply his thoughts rightly that way.

9. It is false that reason discovers them. But how can these men think the use of reason necessary to discover principles that are supposed innate, when reason (if we may believe them) is nothing else but the faculty of deducing unknown truths from principles or propositions that are already known? That certainly can never be thought innate which we have need of reason to discover; unless, as I have said, we will have all the certain truths that reason ever teaches us, to be innate. We may as well think the use of reason necessary to make our eyes discover visible objects, as that there should be need of reason, or the exercise thereof, to make the understanding see what is originally engraved on it, and cannot be in the understanding before it be perceived by it. So that to make reason discover those truths thus imprinted, is to say, that the use of reason discovers to a man what he knew before: and if men have those innate impressed truths originally, and before the use of reason, and yet are always ignorant of them till they come to the use of reason, it is in effect to say, that men know and know them not at the same time.

10. No use made of reasoning in the discovery of these two maxims. It will here perhaps be said that mathematical demonstrations, and other truths that are not innate, are not assented to as soon as proposed, wherein they are distinguished from these maxims and other

innate truths. I shall have occasion to speak of assent upon the first proposing, more particularly by and by. I shall here only, and that very readily, allow, that these maxims and mathematical demonstrations are in this different: that the one have need of reason, using of proofs, to make them out and to gain our assent; but the other, as soon as understood, are, without any the least reasoning, embraced and assented to. But I withal beg leave to observe, that it lays open the weakness of this subterfuge, which requires the use of reason for the discovery of these general truths: since it must be confessed that in their discovery there is no use made of reasoning at all. And I think those who give this answer will not be forward to affirm that the knowledge of this maxim, "That it is impossible for the same thing to be and not to be," is a deduction of our reason. For this would be to destroy that bounty of nature they seem so fond of, whilst they make the knowledge of those principles to depend on the labour of our thoughts. For all reasoning is search, and casting about, and requires pains and application. And how can it with any tolerable sense be supposed, that what was imprinted by nature, as the foundation and guide of our reason, should need the use of reason to discover it?

11. And if there were, this would prove them not innate. Those who will take the pains to reflect with a little attention on the operations of the understanding, will find that this ready assent of the mind to some truths, depends not, either on native inscription, or the use of reason, but on a faculty of the mind quite distinct from both of them, as we shall see hereafter. Reason, therefore, having nothing to do in procuring our assent to these maxims, if by saying, that "men know and assent to them, when they come to the use of reason," be meant, that the use of reason assists us in the knowledge of these maxims, it is utterly false; and were it true, would prove them not to be innate.

12. The coming to the use of reason not the time we come to know these maxims. If by knowing and assenting to them "when we come to the use of reason," be meant, that this is the time when they come to be taken notice of by the mind; and that as soon as children come to the use of reason, they come also to know and assent to these maxims; this also is false and frivolous. First, it is false; because it is evident these maxims are not in the mind so early as the use of reason; and therefore the coming to the use of reason is falsely assigned as the

time of their discovery. How many instances of the use of reason may we observe in children, a long time before they have any knowledge of this maxim, "That it is impossible for the same thing to be and not to be?" And a great part of illiterate people and savages pass many years, even of their rational age, without ever thinking on this and the like general propositions. I grant, men come not to the knowledge of these general and more abstract truths, which are thought innate, till they come to the use of reason; and I add, nor then neither. Which is so, because, till after they come to the use of reason, those general abstract ideas are not framed in the mind, about which those general maxims are, which are mistaken for innate principles, but are indeed discoveries made and verities introduced and brought into the mind by the same way, and discovered by the same steps, as several other propositions, which nobody was ever so extravagant as to suppose innate. This I hope to make plain in the sequel of this Discourse. I allow therefore, a necessity that men should come to the use of reason before they get the knowledge of those general truths; but deny that men's coming to the use of reason is the time of their discovery.

13. By this they are not distinguished from other knowable truths. In the mean time it is observable, that this saying, that men know and assent to these maxims "when they come to the use of reason," amounts in reality of fact to no more but this,- that they are never known nor taken notice of before the use of reason, but may possibly be assented to some time after, during a man's life; but when is uncertain. And so may all other knowable truths, as well as these; which therefore have no advantage nor distinction from others by this note of being known when we come to the use of reason; nor are thereby proved to be innate, but quite the contrary.

14. If coming to the use of reason were the time of their discovery it would not prove them innate. But, secondly, were it true that the precise time of their being known and assented to were, when men come to the use of reason; neither would that prove them innate. This way of arguing is as frivolous as the supposition itself is false. For, by what kind of logic will it appear that any notion is originally by nature imprinted in the mind in its first constitution, because it comes first to be observed and assented to when a faculty of the mind, which has quite a distinct province, begins to exert itself? And therefore the coming to the use of speech, if it were supposed the time that these

maxims are first assented to, (which it may be with as much truth as the time when men come to the use of reason,) would be as good a proof that they were innate, as to say they are innate because men assent to them when they come to the use of reason. I agree then with these men of innate principles, that there is no knowledge of these general and self-evident maxims in the mind, till it comes to the exercise of reason: but I deny that the coming to the use of reason is the precise time when they are first taken notice of, and if that were the precise time, I deny that it would prove them innate. All that can with any truth be meant by this proposition, that men "assent to them when they come to the use of reason," is no more but this,- that the making of general abstract ideas, and the understanding of general names, being a concomitant of the rational faculty, and growing up with it, children commonly get not those general ideas, nor learn the names that stand for them, till, having for a good while exercised their reason about familiar and more particular ideas, they are, by their ordinary discourse and actions with others, acknowledged to be capable of rational conversation. If assenting to these maxims, when men come to the use of reason, can be true in any other sense, I desire it may be shown; or at least, how in this, or any other sense, it proves them innate.

15. The steps by which the mind attains several truths. The senses at first let in particular ideas, and furnish the yet empty cabinet, and the mind by degrees growing familiar with some of them, they are lodged in the memory, and names got to them. Afterwards, the mind proceeding further, abstracts them, and by degrees learns the use of general names. In this manner the mind comes to be furnished with ideas and language, the materials about which to exercise its discursive faculty. And the use of reason becomes daily more visible, as these materials that give it employment increase. But though the having of general ideas and the use of general words and reason usually grow together, yet I see not how this any way proves them innate. The knowledge of some truths, I confess, is very early in the mind but in a way that shows them not to be innate. For, if we will observe, we shall find it still to be about ideas, not innate, but acquired; it being about those first which are imprinted by external things, with which infants have earliest to do, which make the most frequent impressions on their senses. In ideas thus got, the mind discovers that some agree and

others differ, probably as soon as it has any use of memory; as soon as it is able to retain and perceive distinct ideas. But whether it be then or no, this is certain, it does so long before it has the use of words; or comes to that which we commonly call "the use of reason." For a child knows as certainly before it can speak the difference between the ideas of sweet and bitter (i.e. that sweet is not bitter), as it knows afterwards (when it comes to speak) that wormwood and sugarplums are not the same thing.

16. Assent to supposed innate truths depends on having clear and distinct ideas of what their terms mean, and not on their innateness. A child knows not that three and four are equal to seven, till he comes to be able to count seven, and has got the name and idea of equality; and then, upon explaining those words, he presently assents to, or rather perceives the truth of that proposition. But neither does he then readily assent because it is an innate truth, nor was his assent wanting till then because he wanted the use of reason; but the truth of it appears to him as soon as he has settled in his mind the clear and distinct ideas that these names stand for. And then he knows the truth of that proposition upon the same grounds and by the same means, that he knew before that a rod and a cherry are not the same thing; and upon the same grounds also that he may come to know afterwards "That it is impossible for the same thing to be and not to be," as shall be more fully shown hereafter. So that the later it is before any one comes to have those general ideas about which those maxims are; or to know the signification of those general terms that stand for them; or to put together in his mind the ideas they stand for; the later also will it be before he comes to assent to those maxims;- whose terms, with the ideas they stand for, being no more innate than those of a cat or a weasel, he must stay till time and observation have acquainted him with them; and then he will be in a capacity to know the truth of these maxims, upon the first occasion that shall make him put together those ideas in his mind, and observe whether they agree or disagree, according as is expressed in those propositions. And therefore it is that a man knows that eighteen and nineteen are equal to thirty-seven, by the same self-evidence that he knows one and two to be equal to three: yet a child knows this not so soon as the other; not for want of the use of reason, but because the ideas the words eighteen,

nineteen, and thirty-seven stand for, are not so soon got, as those which are signified by one, two, and three.

17. Assenting as soon as proposed and understood, proves them not innate. This evasion therefore of general assent when men come to the use of reason, failing as it does, and leaving no difference between those suppose innate and other truths that are afterwards acquired and learnt, men have endeavoured to secure an universal assent to those they call maxims, by saying, they are generally assented to as soon as proposed, and the terms they are proposed in understood: seeing all men, even children, as soon as they hear and understand the terms, assent to these propositions, they think it is sufficient to prove them innate. For since men never fail after they have once understood the words, to acknowledge them for undoubted truths, they would infer, that certainly these propositions were first lodged in the understanding, which, without any teaching, the mind, at the very first proposal immediately closes with and assents to, and after that never doubts again.

18. If such an assent be·a mark of innate, then "that one and two are equal to three, that sweetness is not bitterness," and a thousand the like, must be innate. In answer to this, I demand whether ready assent given to a proposition, upon first hearing and understanding the terms, be a certain mark of an innate principle? If it be not, such a general assent is in vain urged as a proof of them: if it be said that it is a mark of innate, they must then allow all such propositions to be innate which are generally assented to as soon as heard, whereby they will find themselves plentifully stored with innate principles. For upon the same ground, viz. of assent at first hearing and understanding the terms, that men would have those maxims pass for innate, they must also admit several propositions about numbers to be innate; and thus, that one and two are equal to three, that two and two are equal to four, and a multitude of other the like propositions in numbers, that everybody assents to at first hearing and understanding the terms, must have a place amongst these innate axioms. Nor is this the prerogative of numbers alone, and propositions made about several of them; but even natural philosophy, and all the other sciences, afford propositions which are sure to meet with assent as soon as they are understood. That "two bodies cannot be in the same place" is a truth that nobody any more sticks at than at these maxims, that "it is impossible for the

same thing to be and not to be," that "white is not black," that "a square is not a circle," that "bitterness is not sweetness." These and a million of such other propositions, as many at least as we have distinct ideas of, every man in his wits, at first hearing, and knowing what the names stand for, must necessarily assent to. If these men will be true to their own rule, and have assent at first hearing and understanding the terms to be a mark of innate, they must allow not only as many innate propositions as men have distinct ideas, but as many as men can make propositions wherein different ideas are denied one of another. Since every proposition wherein one different idea is denied of another, will as certainly find assent at first hearing and understanding the terms as this general one, "It is impossible for the same thing to be and not to be," or that which is the foundation of it, and is the easier understood of the two, "The same is not different"; by which account they will have legions of innate propositions of this one sort, without mentioning any other. But, since no proposition can be innate unless the ideas about which it is be innate, this will be to suppose all our ideas of colours, sounds, tastes, figure, &c., innate, than which there cannot be anything more opposite to reason and experience. Universal and ready assent upon hearing and understanding the terms is, I grant, a mark of self-evidence; but self-evidence, depending not on innate impressions, but on something else, (as we shall show hereafter,) belongs to several propositions which nobody was yet so extravagant as to pretend to be innate.

19. Such less general propositions known before these universal maxims. Nor let it be said, that those more particular self-evident propositions, which are assented to at first hearing, as that "one and two are equal to three," that "green is not red," &c., are received as the consequences of those more universal propositions which are looked on as innate principles; since any one, who will but take the pains to observe what passes in the understanding, will certainly find that these, and the like less general propositions, are certainly known, and firmly assented to by those who are utterly ignorant of those more general maxims; and so, being earlier in the mind than those (as they are called) first principles, cannot owe to them the assent wherewith they are received at first hearing.

20. "One and one equal to two, &c., not general nor useful," answered. If it be said, that these propositions, viz. "two and two are

equal to four," "red is not blue," &c., are not general maxims, nor of any great use, I answer, that makes nothing to the argument of universal assent upon hearing and understanding. For, if that be the certain mark of innate, whatever proposition can be found that receives general assent as soon as heard and understood, that must be admitted for an innate proposition, as well as this maxim, "That it is impossible for the same thing to be and not to be," they being upon this ground equal. And as to the difference of being more general, that makes this maxim more remote from being innate; those general and abstract ideas being more strangers to our first apprehensions than those of more particular self-evident propositions; and therefore it is longer before they are admitted and assented to by the growing understanding. And as to the usefulness of these magnified maxims, that perhaps will not be found so great as is generally conceived, when it comes in its due place to be more fully considered.

21. These maxims not being known sometimes till proposed, proves them not innate. But we have not yet done with "assenting to propositions at first hearing and understanding their terms." It is fit we first take notice that this, instead of being a mark that they are innate, is a proof of the contrary; since it supposes that several, who understand and know other things, are ignorant of these principles till they are proposed to them; and that one may be unacquainted with these truths till he hears them from others. For, if they were innate, what need they be proposed in order to gaining assent, when, by being in the understanding, by a natural and original impression, (if there were any such,) they could not but be known before? Or doth the proposing them print them clearer in the mind than nature did? If so, then the consequence will be, that a man knows them better after he has been thus taught them than he did before. Whence it will follow that these principles may be made more evident to us by others' teaching than nature has made them by impression: which will ill agree with the opinion of innate principles, and give but little authority to them; but, on the contrary, makes them unfit to be the foundations of all our other knowledge; as they are pretended to be. This cannot be denied, that men grow first acquainted with many of these self-evident truths upon their being proposed: but it is clear that whosoever does so, finds in himself that he then begins to know a proposition, which he knew not before, and which from thenceforth he never questions;

not because it was innate, but because the consideration of the nature of the things contained in those words would not suffer him to think otherwise, how, or whensoever he is brought to reflect on them. And if whatever is assented to at first hearing and understanding the terms must pass for an innate principle, every well-grounded observation, drawn from particulars into a general rule, must be innate. When yet it is certain that not all, but only sagacious heads, light at first on these observations, and reduce them into general propositions: not innate, but collected from a preceding acquaintance and reflection on particular instances. These, when observing men have made them, unobserving men, when they are proposed to them, cannot refuse their assent to.

22. Implicitly known before proposing, signifies that the mind is capable of understanding them, or else signifies nothing. If it be said, the understanding hath an implicit knowledge of these principles, but not an explicit, before this first hearing (as they must who will say "that they are in the understanding before they are known,") it will be hard to conceive what is meant by a principle imprinted on the understanding implicitly, unless it be this,- that the mind is capable of understanding and assenting firmly to such propositions. And thus all mathematical demonstrations, as well as first principles, must be received as native impressions on the mind; which I fear they will scarce allow them to be, who find it harder to demonstrate a proposition than assent to it when demonstrated. And few mathematicians will be forward to believe, that all the diagrams they have drawn were but copies of those innate characters which nature had engraved upon their minds.

23. The argument of assenting on first hearing, is upon a false supposition of no precedent teaching. There is, I fear, this further weakness in the foregoing argument, which would persuade us that therefore those maxims are to be thought innate, which men admit at first hearing; because they assent to propositions which they are not taught, nor do receive from the force of any argument or demonstration, but a bare explication or understanding of the terms. Under which there seems to me to lie this fallacy, that men are supposed not to be taught nor to learn anything de novo [as an entirely new matter]; when, in truth, they are taught, and do learn something they were ignorant of before. For, first, it is evident that they have

learned the terms, and their signification; neither of which was born with them. But this is not all the acquired knowledge in the case: the ideas themselves, about which the proposition is, are not born with them, no more than their names, but got afterwards. So that in all propositions that are assented to at first hearing, the terms of the proposition, their standing for such ideas, and the ideas themselves that they stand for, being neither of them innate, I would fain know what there is remaining in such propositions that is innate. For I would gladly have any one name that proposition whose terms or ideas were either of them innate. We by degrees get ideas and names, and learn their appropriated connection one with another; and then to propositions made in such terms, whose signification we have learnt, and wherein the agreement or disagreement we can perceive in our ideas when put together is expressed, we at first hearing assent; though to other propositions, in themselves as certain and evident, but which are concerning ideas not so soon or so easily got, we are at the same time no way capable of assenting. For, though a child quickly assents to this proposition, "That an apple is not fire," when by familiar acquaintance he has got the ideas of those two different things distinctly imprinted on his mind, and has learnt that the names apple and fire stand for them; yet it will be some years after, perhaps, before the same child will assent to this proposition, "That it is impossible for the same thing to be and not to be"; because that, though perhaps the words are as easy to be learnt, yet the signification of them being more large, comprehensive, and abstract than of the names annexed to those sensible things the child hath to do with, it is longer before he learns their precise meaning, and it requires more time plainly to form in his mind those general ideas they stand for. Till that be done, you will in vain endeavour to make any child assent to a proposition made up of such general terms; but as soon as ever he has got those ideas, and learned their names, he forwardly closes with the one as well as the other of the forementioned propositions: and with both for the same reason; viz. because he finds the ideas he has in his mind to agree or disagree, according as the words standing for them are affirmed or denied one of another in the proposition. But if propositions be brought to him in words which stand for ideas he has not yet in his mind, to such propositions, however evidently true or false in themselves, he affords neither assent nor dissent, but is ignorant. For words being but empty sounds, any further than they are signs of our ideas, we cannot but assent to them as they correspond to those ideas we have, but no further than that. But the showing by what steps and ways knowledge comes into our minds; and the grounds of several degrees of assent, being the business of the following Discourse, it may suffice to have only touched on it here, as one reason that made me doubt of those innate principles.

24. Not innate, because not universally assented to. To conclude this argument of universal consent, I agree with these defenders of innate principles,- that if they are innate, they must needs have universal assent. For that a truth should be innate and yet not assented to, is to me as unintelligible as for a man to know a truth and be ignorant of it at the same time. But then, by these men's own confession, they cannot be innate; since they are not assented to by those who understand not the terms; nor by a great part of those who do understand them, but have yet never heard nor thought of those propositions; which, I think, is at least one half of mankind. But were the number far less, it would be enough to destroy universal assent, and thereby show these propositions not to be innate, if children alone were ignorant of them.

25. These maxims not the first known. But that I may not be accused to argue from the thoughts of infants, which are unknown to us, and to conclude from what passes in their understandings before they express it; I say next, that these two general propositions are not the truths that first possess the minds of children, nor are antecedent to all acquired and adventitious notions: which, if they were innate, they must needs be. Whether we can determine it or no, it matters not, there is certainly a time when children begin to think, and their words and actions do assure us that they do so. When therefore they are capable of thought, of knowledge, of assent, can it rationally be supposed they can be ignorant of those notions that nature has imprinted, were there any such? Can it be imagined, with any appearance of reason, that they perceive the impressions from things without, and be at the same time ignorant of those characters which nature itself has taken care to stamp within? Can they receive and assent to adventitious notions, and be ignorant of those which are supposed woven into the very principles of their being, and imprinted there in indelible characters, to be the foundation and guide of all their acquired knowledge and future

reasonings? This would be to make nature take pains to no purpose; or at least to write very ill; since its characters could not be read by those eyes which saw other things very well: and those are very ill supposed the clearest parts of truth, and the foundations of all our knowledge, which are not first known, and without which the undoubted knowledge of several other things may be had. The child certainly knows, that the nurse that feeds it is neither the cat it plays with, nor the blackmoor it is afraid of: that the wormseed or mustard it refuses, is not the apple or sugar it cries for: this it is certainly and undoubtedly assured of: but will any one say, it is by virtue of this principle, "That it is impossible for the same thing to be and not to be," that it so firmly assents to these and other parts of its knowledge? Or that the child has any notion or apprehension of that proposition at an age, wherein yet, it is plain, it knows a great many other truths? He that will say, children join in these general abstract speculations with their sucking-bottles and their rattles, may perhaps, with justice, be thought to have more passion and zeal for his opinion, but less sincerity and truth, than one of that age.

26. And so not innate. Though therefore there be several general propositions that meet with constant and ready assent, as soon as proposed to men grown up, who have attained the use of more general and abstract ideas, and names standing for them; yet they not being to be found in those of tender years, who nevertheless know other things, they cannot pretend to universal assent of intelligent persons, and so by no means can be supposed innate;- it being impossible that any truth which is innate (if there were any such) should be unknown, at least to any one who knows anything else. Since, if they are innate truths, they must be innate thoughts: there being nothing a truth in the mind that it has never thought on. Whereby it is evident, if there by any innate truths, they must necessarily be the first of any thought on; the first that appear.

27. Not innate, because they appear least where what is innate shows itself clearest. That the general maxims we are discoursing of are not known to children, idiots, and a great part of mankind, we have already sufficiently proved: whereby it is evident they have not an universal assent, nor are general impressions. But there is this further argument in it against their being innate: that these characters, if they were native and original impressions, should appear fairest and

clearest in those persons in whom yet we find no footsteps of them; and it is, in my opinion, a strong presumption that they are not innate, since they are least known to those in whom, if they were innate, they must needs exert themselves with most force and vigour. For children, idiots, savages, and illiterate people, being of all others the least corrupted by custom, or borrowed opinions; learning and education having not cast their native thoughts into new moulds; nor by super-inducing foreign and studied doctrines, confounded those fair characters nature had written there; one might reasonably imagine that in their minds these innate notions should lie open fairly to every one's view, as it is certain the thoughts of children do. It might very well be expected that these principles should be perfectly known to naturals; which being stamped immediately on the soul, (as these men suppose,) can have no dependence on the constitution or organs of the body, the only confessed difference between them and others. One would think, according to these men's principles, that all these native beams of light (were there any such) should, in those who have no reserves, no arts of concealment, shine out in their full lustre, and leave us in no more doubt of their being there, than we are of their love of pleasure and abhorrence of pain. But alas, amongst children, idiots, savages, and the grossly illiterate, what general maxims are to be found? What universal principles of knowledge? Their notions are few and narrow, borrowed only from those objects they have had most to do with, and which have made upon their senses the frequentest and strongest impressions. A child knows his nurse and his cradle, and by degrees the playthings of a little more advanced age; and a young savage has, perhaps, his head filled with love and hunting, according to the fashion of his tribe. But he that from a child untaught, or a wild inhabitant of the woods, will expect these abstract maxims and reputed principles of science, will, I fear, find himself mistaken. Such kind of general propositions are seldom mentioned in the huts of Indians: much less are they to be found in the thoughts of children, or any impressions of them on the minds of naturals. They are the language and business of the schools and academies of learned nations, accustomed to that sort of conversation or learning, where disputes are frequent; these maxims being suited to artificial argumentation and useful for conviction, but not much conducing to the discovery of truth or advancement of knowledge. But of their small use for the improvement of knowledge I shall have occasion to speak more at large.

28. Recapitulation. I know not how absurd this may seem to the masters of demonstration. And probably it will hardly go down with anybody at first hearing. I must therefore beg a little truce with prejudice, and the forbearance of censure, till I have been heard out in the sequel of this Discourse, being very willing to submit to better judgements. And since I impartially search after truth, I shall not be sorry to be convinced, that I have been too fond of my own notions; which I confess we are all apt to be, when application and study have warmed our heads with them.

Upon the whole matter, I cannot see any ground to think these two speculative Maxims innate: since they are not universally assented to; and the assent they so generally find is no other than what several propositions, not allowed to be innate, equally partake in with them: and since the assent that is given them is produced another way, and comes not from natural inscription, as I doubt not but to make appear in the following Discourse. And if these "first principles" of knowledge and science are found not to be innate, no other speculative maxims can (I suppose), with better right pretend to be so.

Of Simple Ideas

1. Uncompounded appearances. The better to understand the nature, manner, and extent of our knowledge, one thing is carefully to be observed concerning the ideas we have; and that is, that some of them are simple and some complex.

Though the qualities that affect our senses are, in the things themselves, so united and blended, that there is no separation, no distance between them; yet it is plain, the ideas they produce in the mind enter by the senses simple and unmixed. For, though the sight and touch often take in from the same object, at the same time, different ideas;- as a man sees at once motion and colour; the hand feels softness and warmth in the same piece of wax: yet the simple ideas thus united in the same subject, are as perfectly distinct as those that come in by different senses. The coldness and hardness which a man feels in a piece of ice being as distinct ideas in the mind as the smell and whiteness of a lily; or as the taste of sugar, and smell of a rose. And there is nothing can be plainer to a man than the clear and distinct perception he has of those simple ideas; which, being each in itself uncompounded, contains in it nothing but one uniform appearance, or conception in the mind, and is not distinguishable into different ideas.

2. The mind can neither make nor destroy them. These simple ideas, the materials of all our knowledge, are suggested and furnished to the mind only by those two ways above mentioned, viz. sensation and reflection. When the understanding is once stored with these simple ideas, it has the power to repeat, compare, and unite them, even to an almost infinite variety, and so can make at pleasure new complex ideas. But it is not in the power of the most exalted wit, or enlarged understanding, by any quickness or variety of thought, to invent or frame one new simple idea in the mind, not taken in by the ways before mentioned: nor can any force of the understanding destroy those that are there. The dominion of man, in this little world of his own understanding being much the same as it is in the great world of visible things; wherein his power, however managed by art and skill, reaches no farther than to compound and divide the materials that are made to his hand; but can do nothing towards the making the least particle of new matter, or destroying one atom of what is already in being. The same inability will every one find in himself, who shall go about to fashion in his understanding one simple idea, not received in by his senses from external objects, or by reflection from the operations of his own mind about them. I would have any one try to fancy any taste which had never affected his palate; or frame the idea of a scent he had never smelt: and when he can do this, I will also conclude that a blind man hath ideas of colours, and a deaf man true distinct notions of sounds.

3. Only the qualities that affect the senses are imaginable. This is the reason why, though we cannot believe it impossible to God to make a creature with other organs, and more ways to convey into the understanding the notice of corporeal things than those five, as they are usually counted, which he has given to man- yet I think it is not possible for any man to imagine any other qualities in bodies, howsoever constituted, whereby they can be taken notice of, besides sounds, tastes, smells, visible and tangible qualities. And had mankind been made but with four senses, the qualities then which are the objects of the fifth sense had been as far from our notice, imagination, and conception, as now any belonging to a sixth, seventh, or eighth

sense can possibly be;- which, whether yet some other creatures, in some other parts of this vast and stupendous universe, may not have, will be a great presumption to deny. He that will not set himself proudly at the top of all things, but will consider the immensity of this fabric, and the great variety that is to be found in this little and inconsiderable part of it which he has to do with, may be apt to think that, in other mansions of it, there may be other and different intelligent beings, of whose faculties he has as little knowledge or apprehension as a worm shut up in one drawer of a cabinet hath of the senses or understanding of a man; such variety and excellency being suitable to the wisdom and power of the Maker. I have here followed the common opinion of man's having but five senses; though, perhaps, there may be justly counted more;- but either supposition serves equally to my present purpose.

Of Simple Ideas of Sense

1. Division of simple ideas. The better to conceive the ideas we receive from sensation, it may not be amiss for us to consider them, in reference to the different ways whereby they make their approaches to our minds, and make themselves perceivable by us.

First, then, There are some which come into our minds by one sense only.

Secondly, There are others that convey themselves into the mind by more senses than one.

Thirdly, Others that are had from reflection only.

Fourthly, There are some that make themselves way, and are suggested to the mind by all the ways of sensation and reflection.

We shall consider them apart under these several heads.

Ideas of one sense. There are some ideas which have admittance only through one sense, which is peculiarly adapted to receive them. Thus light and colours, as white, red, yellow, blue; with their several degrees or shades and mixtures, as green, scarlet, purple, sea-green, and the rest, come in only by the eyes. All kinds of noises, sounds, and tones, only by the ears. The several tastes and smells, by the nose and palate. And if these organs, or the nerves which are the conduits to convey them from without to their audience in the brain,- the mind's presence-room (as I may so call it)- are any of them so disordered as not to perform their functions, they have no postern to be admitted by; no other way to bring themselves into view, and be perceived by the understanding.

The most considerable of those belonging to the touch, are heat and cold, and solidity: all the rest, consisting almost wholly in the sensible configuration, as smooth and rough; or else, more or less firm adhesion of the parts, as hard and soft, tough and brittle, are obvious enough.

2. Few simple ideas have names. I think it will be needless to enumerate all the particular simple ideas belonging to each sense. Nor indeed is it possible if we would; there being a great many more of them belonging to most of the senses than we have names for. The variety of smells, which are as many almost, if not more, than species of bodies in the world, do most of them want names. Sweet and stinking commonly serve our turn for these ideas, which in effect is little more than to call them pleasing or displeasing; though the smell of a rose and violet, both sweet, are certainly very distinct ideas. Nor are the different tastes, that by our palates we receive ideas of, much better provided with names. Sweet, bitter, sour, harsh, and salt are almost all the epithets we have to denominate that numberless variety of relishes, which are to be found distinct, not only in almost every sort of creatures, but in the different parts of the same plant, fruit, or animal. The same may be said of colours and sounds. I shall, therefore, in the account of simple ideas I am here giving, content myself to set down only such as are most material to our present purpose, or are in themselves less apt to be taken notice of though they are very frequently the ingredients of our complex ideas; amongst which, I think, I may well account solidity, which therefore I shall treat of in the next chapter.

Idea of Solidity

1. We receive this idea from touch. The idea of solidity we receive by our touch: and it arises from the resistance which we find in body to the entrance of any other body into the place it possesses, till it has left it. There is no idea which we receive more constantly from sensation than solidity. Whether we move or rest, in what posture soever we are, we always feel something under us that support us, and hinders our further sinking downwards; and the bodies which we daily handle make us perceive that, whilst they remain between them, they do, by an insurmountable force, hinder the approach of the parts of our

hands that press them. That which thus hinders the approach of two bodies, when they are moved one towards another, I call solidity. I will not dispute whether this acceptation of the word solid be nearer to its original signification than that which mathematicians use it in. It suffices that I think the common notion of solidity will allow, if not justify, this use of it; but if any one think it better to call it impenetrability, he has my consent. Only I have thought the term solidity the more proper to express this idea, not only because of its vulgar use in that sense, but also because it carries something more of positive in it than impenetrability; which is negative, and is perhaps more a consequence of solidity, than solidity itself. This, of all other, seems the idea most intimately connected with, and essential to body; so as nowhere else to be found or imagined, but only in matter. And though our senses take no notice of it, but in masses of matter, of a bulk sufficient to cause a sensation in us: yet the mind, having once got this idea from such grosser sensible bodies, traces it further, and considers it, as well as figure, in the minutest particle of matter that can exist; and finds it inseparably inherent in body, wherever or however modified.

2. Solidity fills space. This is the idea which belongs to body, whereby we conceive it to fill space. The idea of which filling of space is,- that where we imagine any space taken up by a solid substance, we conceive it so to possess it, that it excludes all other solid substances; and will for ever hinder any other two bodies, that move towards one another in a straight line, from coming to touch one another, unless it removes from between them in a line not parallel to that which they move in. This idea of it, the bodies which we ordinarily handle sufficiently furnish us with.

3. Distinct from space. This resistance, whereby it keeps other bodies out of the space which it possesses, is so great, that no force, how great soever, can surmount it. All the bodies in the world, pressing a drop of water on all sides, will never be able to overcome the resistance which it will make, soft as it is, to their approaching one another, till it be removed out of their way: whereby our idea of solidity is distinguished both from pure space, which is capable neither of resistance nor motion; and from the ordinary idea of hardness. For a man may conceive two bodies at a distance, so as they may approach one another, without touching or displacing any solid thing, till their

superficies come to meet; whereby, I think, we have the clear idea of space without solidity. For (not to go so far as annihilation of any particular body) I ask, whether a man cannot have the idea of the motion of one single body alone, without any other succeeding immediately into its place? I think it is evident he can: the idea of motion in one body no more including the idea of motion in another, than the idea of a square figure in one body includes the idea of a square figure in another. I do not ask, whether bodies do so exist, that the motion of one body cannot really be without the motion of another. To determine this either way, is to beg the question for or against a vacuum. But my question is,- whether one cannot have the idea of one body moved, whilst others are at rest? And I think this no one will deny. If so, then the place it deserted gives us the idea of pure space without solidity; whereinto any other body may enter, without either resistance or protrusion of anything. When the sucker in a pump is drawn, the space it filled in the tube is certainly the same whether any other body follows the motion of the sucker or not: nor does it imply a contradiction that, upon the motion of one body, another that is only contiguous to it should not follow it. The necessity of such a motion is built only on the supposition that the world is full; but not on the distinct ideas of space and solidity, which are as different as resistance and not resistance, protrusion and not protrusion. And that men have ideas of space without a body, their very disputes about a vacuum plainly demonstrate, as is shown in another place.

4. From hardness. Solidity is hereby also differenced from hardness, in that solidity consists in repletion, and so an utter exclusion of other bodies out of the space it possesses: but hardness, in a firm cohesion of the parts of matter, making up masses of a sensible bulk, so that the whole does not easily change its figure. And indeed, hard and soft are names that we give to things only in relation to the constitutions of our own bodies; that being generally called hard by us, which will put us to pain sooner than change figure by the pressure of any part of our bodies; and that, on the contrary, soft, which changes the situation of its parts upon an easy and unpainful touch.

But this difficulty of changing the situation of the sensible parts amongst themselves, or of the figure of the whole, gives no more solidity to the hardest body in the world than to the softest; nor is an adamant one jot more solid than water. For, though the two flat sides of two pieces of marble will more easily approach each other, between which there is nothing but water or air, than if there be a diamond between them; yet it is not that the parts of the diamond are more solid than those of water, or resist more; but because the parts of water, being more easily separable from each other, they will, by a side motion, be more easily removed, and give way to the approach of the two pieces of marble. But if they could be kept from making place by that side motion, they would eternally hinder the approach of these two pieces of marble, as much as the diamond; and it would be as impossible by any force to surmount their resistance, as to surmount the resistance of the parts of a diamond. The softest body in the world will as invincibly resist the coming together of any other two bodies, if it be not put out of the way, but remain between them, as the hardest that can be found or imagined. He that shall fill a yielding soft body well with air or water, will quickly find its resistance. And he that thinks that nothing but bodies that are hard can keep his hands from approaching one another, may be pleased to make a trial, with the air inclosed in a football. The experiment, I have been told, was made at Florence, with a hollow globe of gold filled with water, and exactly closed; which further shows the solidity of so soft a body as water. For the golden globe thus filled, being put into a press, which was driven by the extreme force of screws, the water made itself way through the pores of that very close metal, and finding no room for a nearer approach of its particles within, got to the outside, where it rose like a dew, and so fell in drops, before the sides of the globe could be made to yield to the violent compression of the engine that squeezed it.

5. On solidity depend impulse, resistance, and protrusion. By this idea of solidity is the extension of body distinguished from the extension of space:- the extension of body being nothing but the cohesion or continuity of solid, separable, movable parts; and the extension of space, the continuity of unsolid, inseparable, and immovable parts. Upon the solidity of bodies also depend their mutual impulse, resistance, and protrusion. Of pure space then, and solidity, there are several (amongst which I confess myself one) who persuade themselves they have clear and distinct ideas; and that they can think on space, without anything in it that resists or is protruded by body. This is the idea of pure space, which they think they have as clear as any idea they can have of the extension of body: the idea of the

distance between the opposite parts of a concave superficies being equally as clear without as with the idea of any solid parts between: and on the other side, they persuade themselves that they have, distinct from that of pure space, the idea of something that fills space, that can be protruded by the impulse of other bodies, or resist their motion. If there be others that have not these two ideas distinct, but confound them, and make but one of them, I know not how men, who have the same idea under different names, or different ideas under the same name, can in that case talk with one another; any more than a man who, not being blind or deaf, has distinct ideas of the colour of scarlet and the sound of a trumpet, could discourse concerning scarlet colour with the blind man I mentioned in another place, who fancied that the idea of scarlet was like the sound of a trumpet.

6. What solidity is. If any one ask me, What this solidity is, I send him to his senses to inform him. Let him put a flint or a football between his hands, and then endeavour to join them, and he will know. If he thinks this not a sufficient explication of solidity, what it is, and wherein it consists; I promise to tell him what it is, and wherein it consists, when he tells me what thinking is, or wherein it consists; or explains to me what extension or motion is, which perhaps seems much easier. The simple ideas we have, are such as experience teaches them us; but if, beyond that, we endeavour by words to make them clearer in the mind, we shall succeed no better than if we went about to clear up the darkness of a blind man's mind by talking; and to discourse into him the ideas of light and colours. The reason of this I shall show in another place.

Of Simple Ideas of Divers Senses

Ideas received both by seeing and touching. The ideas we get by more than one sense are, of space or extension, figure, rest, and motion. For these make perceivable impressions, both on the eyes and touch; and we can receive and convey into our minds the ideas of the extension, figure, motion, and rest of bodies, both by seeing and feeling. But having occasion to speak more at large of these in another place, I here only enumerate them.

Of Simple Ideas of Reflection

1. Simple ideas are the operations of mind about its other ideas. The mind receiving the ideas mentioned in the foregoing chapters from without, when it turns its view inward upon itself, and observes its own

actions about those ideas it has, takes from thence other ideas, which are as capable to be the objects of its contemplation as any of those it received from foreign things.

2. The idea of perception, and idea of willing, we have from reflection. The two great and principal actions of the mind, which are most frequently considered, and which are so frequent that every one that pleases may take notice of them in himself, are these two:-

Perception, or Thinking; and
Volition, or Willing.

The power of thinking is called the Understanding, and the power of volition is called the Will; and these two powers or abilities in the mind are denominated faculties.

Of some of the modes of these simple ideas of reflection, such as are remembrance, discerning, reasoning, judging, knowledge, faith, &c., I shall have occasion to speak hereafter.

Of Simple Ideas of both Sensation and Reflection

1. Ideas of pleasure and pain. There be other simple ideas which convey themselves into the mind by all the ways of sensation and reflection, viz. pleasure or delight, and its opposite, pain, or uneasiness; power; existence; unity.

2. Mix with almost all our other ideas. Delight or uneasiness, one or other of them, join themselves to almost all our ideas both of sensation and reflection: and there is scarce any affection of our senses from without, any retired thought of our mind within, which is not able to produce in us pleasure or pain. By pleasure and pain, I would be understood to signify, whatsoever delights or molests us; whether it arises from the thoughts of our minds, or anything operating on our bodies. For, whether we call it satisfaction, delight, pleasure, happiness, &c., on the one side, or uneasiness, trouble, pain, torment, anguish, misery, &c., on the other, they are still but different degrees of the same thing, and belong to the ideas of pleasure and pain, delight or uneasiness; which are the names I shall most commonly use for those two sorts of ideas.

3. As motives of our actions. The infinite wise Author of our being, having given us the power over several parts of our bodies, to move or keep them at rest as we think fit; and also. by the motion of them, to move ourselves and other contiguous bodies, in which consist all the actions of our body: having also given a power to our minds, in

several instances, to choose, amongst its ideas, which it will think on, and to pursue the inquiry of this or that subject with consideration and attention, to excite us to these actions of thinking and motion that we are capable of,- has been pleased to join to several thoughts, and several sensations a perception of delight. If this were wholly separated from all our outward sensations, and inward thoughts, we should have no reason to prefer one thought or action to another; negligence to attention, or motion to rest. And so we should neither stir our bodies, nor employ our minds, but let our thoughts (if I may so call it) run adrift, without any direction or design, and suffer the ideas of our minds, like unregarded shadows, to make their appearances there, as it happened, without attending to them. In which state man, however furnished with the faculties of understanding and will, would be a very idle, inactive creature, and pass his time only in a lazy, lethargic dream. It has therefore pleased our wise Creator to annex to several objects, and the ideas which we receive from them, as also to several of our thoughts, a concomitant pleasure, and that in several objects, to several degrees, that those faculties which he had endowed us with might not remain wholly idle and unemployed by us.

4. An end and use of pain. Pain has the same efficacy and use to set us on work that pleasure has, we being as ready to employ our faculties to avoid that, as to pursue this: only this is worth our consideration, that pain is often produced by the same objects and ideas that produce pleasure in us. This their near conjunction, which makes us often feel pain in the sensations where we expected pleasure, gives us new occasion of admiring the wisdom and goodness of our Maker, who, designing the preservation of our being, has annexed pain to the application of many things to our bodies, to warn us of the harm that they will do, and as advices to withdraw from them. But he, not designing our preservation barely, but the preservation of every part and organ in its perfection, hath in many cases annexed pain to those very ideas which delight us. Thus heat, that is very agreeable to us in one degree, by a little greater increase of it proves no ordinary torment: and the most pleasant of all sensible objects, light itself, if there be too much of it, if increased beyond a due proportion to our eyes, causes a very painful sensation. Which is wisely and favourably so ordered by nature, that when any object does, by the vehemency of its operation, disorder the instruments of sensation, whose structures

cannot but be very nice and delicate, we might, by the pain, be warned to withdraw, before the organ be quite put out of order, and so be unfitted for its proper function for the future. The consideration of those objects that produce it may well persuade us, that this is the end or use of pain. For, though great light be insufferable to our eyes, yet the highest degree of darkness does not at all disease them: because that, causing no disorderly motion in it, leaves that curious organ unharmed in its natural state. But yet excess of cold as well as heat pains us: because it is equally destructive to that temper which is necessary to the preservation of life, and the exercise of the several functions of the body, and which consists in a moderate degree of warmth; or, if you please, a motion of the insensible parts of our bodies, confined within certain bounds.

5. Another end. Beyond all this, we may find another reason why God hath scattered up and down several degrees of pleasure and pain, in all the things that environ and affect us; and blended them together in almost all that our thoughts and senses have to do with;- that we, finding imperfection, dissatisfaction, and want of complete happiness, in all the enjoyments which the creatures can afford us, might be led to seek it in the enjoyment of Him with whom there is fullness of joy, and at whose right hand are pleasures for evermore.

6. Goodness of God in annexing pleasure and pain to our other ideas. Though what I have here said may not, perhaps, make the ideas of pleasure and pain clearer to us than our own experience does, which is the only way that we are capable of having them; yet the consideration of the reason why they are annexed to so many other ideas, serving to give us due sentiments of the wisdom and goodness of the Sovereign Disposer of all things, may not be unsuitable to the main end of these inquiries: the knowledge and veneration of him being the chief end of all our thoughts, and the proper business of all understandings.

7. Ideas of existence and unity. Existence and Unity are two other ideas that are suggested to the understanding by every object without, and every idea within. When ideas are in our minds, we consider them as being actually there, as well as we consider things to be actually without us;- which is, that they exist, or have existence. And whatever we can consider as one thing, whether a real being or idea, suggests to the understanding the idea of unity.

8. Idea of power. Power also is another of those simple ideas which we receive from sensation and reflection. For, observing in ourselves that we do and can think, and that we can at pleasure move several parts of our bodies which were at rest; the effects, also, that natural bodies are able to produce in one another, occurring every moment to our senses,- we both these ways get the idea of power.

9. Idea of succession. Besides these there is another idea, which, though suggested by our senses, yet is more constantly offered to us by what passes in our minds; and that is the idea of succession. For if we look immediately into ourselves, and reflect on what is observable there, we shall find our ideas always, whilst we are awake, or have any thought, passing in train, one going and another coming, without intermission.

10. Simple ideas the materials of all our knowledge. These, if they are not all, are at least (as I think) the most considerable of those simple ideas which the mind has, and out of which is made all its other knowledge; all which it receives only by the two forementioned ways of sensation and reflection.

Nor let any one think these too narrow bounds for the capacious mind of man to expatiate in, which takes its flight further than the stars, and cannot be confined by the limits of the world; that extends its thoughts often even beyond the utmost expansion of Matter, and makes excursions into that incomprehensible Inane. I grant all this, but desire any one to assign any simple idea which is not received from one of those inlets before mentioned, or any complex idea not made out of those simple ones. Nor will it be so strange to think these few simple ideas sufficient to employ the quickest thought, or largest capacity; and to furnish the materials of all that various knowledge, and more various fancies and opinions of all mankind, if we consider how many words may be made out of the various composition of twenty-four letters; or if, going one step further, we will but reflect on the variety of combinations that may be made with barely one of the above-mentioned ideas, viz. number, whose stock is inexhaustible and truly infinite: and what a large and immense field doth extension alone afford the mathematicians?

Some further considerations concerning our Simple Ideas of Sensation

1. Positive ideas from privative causes. Concerning the simple ideas of Sensation, it is to be considered,- that whatsoever is so

constituted in nature as to be able, by affecting our senses, to cause any perception in the mind, doth thereby produce in the understanding a simple idea; which, whatever be the external cause of it, when it comes to be taken notice of by our discerning faculty, it is by the mind looked on and considered there to be a real positive idea in the understanding, as much as any other whatsoever; though, perhaps, the cause of it be but a privation of the subject.

2. Ideas in the mind distinguished from that in things which gives rise to them. Thus the ideas of heat and cold, light and darkness, white and black, motion and rest, are equally clear and positive ideas in the mind; though, perhaps, some of the causes which produce them are barely privations, in those subjects from whence our senses derive those ideas. These the understanding, in its view of them, considers all as distinct positive ideas, without taking notice of the causes that produce them: which is an inquiry not belonging to the idea, as it is in the understanding, but to the nature of the things existing without us. These are two very different things, and carefully to be distinguished; it being one thing to perceive and know the idea of white or black, and quite another to examine what kind of particles they must be, and how ranged in the superficies, to make any object appear white or black.

3. We may have the ideas when we are ignorant of their physical causes. A painter or dyer who never inquired into their causes hath the ideas of white and black, and other colours, as clearly, perfectly, and distinctly in his understanding, and perhaps more distinctly, than the philosopher who hath busied himself in considering their natures, and thinks he knows how far either of them is, in its cause, positive or privative; and the idea of black is no less positive in his mind than that of white, however the cause of that colour in the external object may be only a privation.

4. Why a privative cause in nature may occasion a positive idea. If it were the design of my present undertaking to inquire into the natural causes and manner of perception, I should offer this as a reason why a privative cause might, in some cases at least, produce a positive idea; viz. that all sensation being produced in us only by different degrees and modes of motion in our animal spirits, variously agitated by external objects, the abatement of any former motion must as necessarily produce a new sensation as the variation or increase of it;

and so introduce a new idea, which depends only on a different motion of the animal spirits in that organ.

5. Negative names need not be meaningless. But whether this be so or not I will not here determine, but appeal to every one's own experience, whether the shadow of a man, though it consists of nothing but the absence of light (and the more the absence of light is, the more discernible is the shadow) does not, when a man looks on it, cause as clear and positive idea in his mind as a man himself, though covered over with clear sunshine? And the picture of a shadow is a positive thing. Indeed, we have negative names, which stand not directly for positive ideas, but for their absence, such as insipid, silence, nihil [nothing], &c.; which words denote positive ideas, v.g. [namely, in a word] taste, sound, being, with a signification of their absence.

6. Whether any ideas are due to causes really privative. And thus one may truly be said to see darkness. For, supposing a hole perfectly dark, from whence no light is reflected, it is certain one may see the figure of it, or it may be painted; or whether the ink I write with makes any other idea, is a question. The privative causes I have here assigned of positive ideas are according to the common opinion; but, in truth, it will be hard to determine whether there be really any ideas from a privative cause, till it be determined, whether rest be any more a privation than motion.

7. Ideas in the mind, qualities in bodies. To discover the nature of our ideas the better, and to discourse of them intelligibly, it will be convenient to distinguish them as they are ideas or perceptions in our minds; and as they are modifications of matter in the bodies that cause such perceptions in us: that so we may not think (as perhaps usually is done) that they are exactly the images and resemblances of something inherent in the subject; most of those of sensation being in the mind no more the likeness of something existing without us, than the names that stand for them are the likeness of our ideas, which yet upon hearing they are apt to excite in us.

8. Our ideas and the qualities of bodies. Whatsoever the mind perceives in itself, or is the immediate object of perception, thought, or understanding, that I call idea; and the power to produce any idea in our mind, I call quality of the subject wherein that power is. Thus a snowball having the power to produce in us the ideas of white, cold, and round,- the power to produce those ideas in us, as they are in the

snowball, I call qualities; and as they are sensations or perceptions in our understandings, I call them ideas; which ideas, if I speak of sometimes as in the things themselves, I would be understood to mean those qualities in the objects which produce them in us.

9. Primary qualities of bodies. Qualities thus considered in bodies are,

First, such as are utterly inseparable from the body, in what state soever it be; and such as in all the alterations and changes it suffers, all the force can be used upon it, it constantly keeps; and such as sense constantly finds in every particle of matter which has bulk enough to be perceived; and the mind finds inseparable from every particle of matter, though less than to make itself singly be perceived by our senses: v.g. Take a grain of wheat, divide it into two parts; each part has still solidity, extension, figure, and mobility: divide it again, and it retains still the same qualities; and so divide it on, till the parts become insensible; they must retain still each of them all those qualities. For division (which is all that a mill, or pestle, or any other body, does upon another, in reducing it to insensible parts) can never take away either solidity, extension, figure, or mobility from any body, but only makes two or more distinct separate masses of matter, of that which was but one before; all which distinct masses, reckoned as so many distinct bodies, after division, make a certain number. These I call original or primary qualities of body, which I think we may observe to produce simple ideas in us, viz. solidity, extension, figure, motion or rest, and number.

10. Secondary qualities of bodies. Secondly, such qualities which in truth are nothing in the objects themselves but power to produce various sensations in us by their primary qualities, i.e. by the bulk, figure, texture, and motion of their insensible parts, as colours, sounds, tastes, &c. These I call secondary qualities. To these might be added a third sort, which are allowed to be barely powers; though they are as much real qualities in the subject as those which I, to comply with the common way of speaking, call qualities, but for distinction, secondary qualities. For the power in fire to produce a new colour, or consistency, in wax or clay,- by its primary qualities, is as much a quality in fire, as the power it has to produce in me a new idea or sensation of warmth or burning, which I felt not before,- by the same

primary qualities, viz. the bulk, texture, and motion of its insensible parts.

11. How bodies produce ideas in us. The next thing to be considered is, how bodies produce ideas in us; and that is manifestly by impulse, the only way which we can conceive bodies to operate in.

12. By motions, external, and in our organism. If then external objects be not united to our minds when they produce ideas therein; and yet we perceive these original qualities in such of them as singly fall under our senses, it is evident that some motion must be thence continued by our nerves, or animal spirits, by some parts of our bodies, to the brains or the seat of sensation, there to produce in our minds the particular ideas we have of them. And since the extension, figure, number, and motion of bodies of an observable bigness, may be perceived at a distance by the sight, it is evident some singly imperceptible bodies must come from them to the eyes, and thereby convey to the brain some motion; which produces these ideas which we have of them in us.

13. How secondary qualities produce their ideas. After the same manner, that the ideas of these original qualities are produced in us, we may conceive that the ideas of secondary qualities are also produced, viz. by the operation of insensible particles on our senses. For, it being manifest that there are bodies and good store of bodies, each whereof are so small, that we cannot by any of our senses discover either their bulk, figure, or motion,- as is evident in the particles of the air and water, and others extremely smaller than those; perhaps as much smaller than the particles of air and water, as the particles of air and water are smaller than peas or hail-stones;- let us suppose at present that the different motions and figures, bulk and number, of such particles, affecting the several organs of our senses, produce in us those different sensations which we have from the colours and smells of bodies; v.g. that a violet, by the impulse of such insensible particles of matter, of peculiar figures and bulks, and in different degrees and modifications of their motions, causes the ideas of the blue colour, and sweet scent of that flower to be produced in our minds. It being no more impossible to conceive that God should annex such ideas to such motions, with which they have no similitude, than that he should annex the idea of pain to the motion of a piece of steel dividing our flesh, with which that idea hath no resemblance.

14. They depend on the primary qualities. What I have said concerning colours and smells may be understood also of tastes and sounds, and other the like sensible qualities; which, whatever reality we by mistake attribute to them, are in truth nothing in the objects themselves, but powers to produce various sensations in us; and depend on those primary qualities, viz. bulk, figure, texture, and motion of parts as I have said.

15. Ideas of primary qualities are resemblances; of secondary, not. From whence I think it easy to draw this observation,- that the ideas of primary qualities of bodies are resemblances of them, and their patterns do really exist in the bodies themselves, but the ideas produced in us by these secondary qualities have no resemblance of them at all. There is nothing like our ideas, existing in the bodies themselves. They are, in the bodies we denominate from them, only a power to produce those sensations in us: and what is sweet, blue, or warm in idea, is but the certain bulk, figure, and motion of the insensible parts, in the bodies themselves, which we call so.

16. Examples. Flame is denominated hot and light; snow, white and cold; and manna, white and sweet, from the ideas they produce in us. Which qualities are commonly thought to be the same in those bodies that those ideas are in us, the one the perfect resemblance of the other, as they are in a mirror, and it would by most men be judged very extravagant if one should say otherwise. And yet he that will consider that the same fire that, at one distance produces in us the sensation of warmth, does, at a nearer approach, produce in us the far different sensation of pain, ought to bethink himself what reason he has to say- that this idea of warmth, which was produced in him by the fire, is actually in the fire; and his idea of pain, which the same fire produced in him the same way, is not in the fire. Why are whiteness and coldness in snow, and pain not, when it produces the one and the other idea in us; and can do neither, but by the bulk, figure, number, and motion of its solid parts?

17. The ideas of the primary alone really exist. The particular bulk, number, figure, and motion of the parts of fire or snow are really in them,- whether any one's senses perceive them or no: and therefore they may be called real qualities, because they really exist in those bodies. But light, heat, whiteness, or coldness, are no more really in them than sickness or pain is in manna. Take away the sensation of

them; let not the eyes see light or colours, nor the ears hear sounds; let the palate not taste, nor the nose smell, and all colours, tastes, odours, and sounds, as they are such particular ideas, vanish and cease, and are reduced to their causes, i.e. bulk, figure, and motion of parts.

18. The secondary exist in things only as modes of the primary. A piece of manna of a sensible bulk is able to produce in us the idea of a round or square figure; and by being removed from one place to another, the idea of motion. This idea of motion represents it as it really is in manna moving: a circle or square are the same, whether in idea or existence, in the mind or in the manna. And this, both motion and figure, are really in the manna, whether we take notice of them or no: this everybody is ready to agree to. Besides, manna, by tie bulk, figure, texture, and motion of its parts, has a power to produce the sensations of sickness, and sometimes of acute pains or gripings in us. That these ideas of sickness and pain are not in the manna, but effects of its operations on us, and are nowhere when we feel them not; this also every one readily agrees to. And yet men are hardly to be brought to think that sweetness and whiteness are not really in manna; which are but the effects of the operations of manna, by the motion, size, and figure of its particles, on the eyes and palate: as the pain and sickness caused by manna are confessedly nothing but the effects of its operations on the stomach and guts, by the size, motion, and figure of its insensible parts, (for by nothing else can a body operate, as has been proved): as if it could not operate on the eyes and palate, and thereby produce in the mind particular distinct ideas, which in itself it has not, as well as we allow it can operate on the guts and stomach, and thereby produce distinct ideas, which in itself it has not. These ideas, being all effects of the operations of manna on several parts of our bodies, by the size, figure number, and motion of its parts;- why those produced by the eyes and palate should rather be thought to be really in the manna, than those produced by the stomach and guts; or why the pain and sickness, ideas that are the effect of manna, should be thought to be nowhere when they are not felt; and yet the sweetness and whiteness, effects of the same manna on other parts of the body, by ways equally as unknown, should be thought to exist in the manna, when they are not seen or tasted, would need some reason to explain.

19. Examples. Let us consider the red and white colours in porphyry. Hinder light from striking on it, and its colours vanish; it no longer produces any such ideas in us: upon the return of light it produces these appearances on us again. Can any one think any real alterations are made in the porphyry by the presence or absence of light; and that those ideas of whiteness and redness are really in porphyry in the light, when it is plain it has no colour in the dark? It has, indeed, such a configuration of particles, both night and day, as are apt, by the rays of light rebounding from some parts of that hard stone, to produce in us the idea of redness, and from others the idea of whiteness; but whiteness or redness are not in it at any time, but such a texture that hath the power to produce such a sensation in us.

20. Pound an almond, and the clear white colour will be altered into a dirty one, and the sweet taste into an oily one. What real alteration can the beating of the pestle make in any body, but an alteration of the texture of it?

21. Explains how water felt as cold by one hand may be warm to the other. Ideas being thus distinguished and understood, we may be able to give an account how the same water, at the same time, may produce the idea of cold by one hand and of heat by the other: whereas it is impossible that the same water, if those ideas were really in it, should at the same time be both hot and cold. For, if we imagine warmth, as it is in our hands, to be nothing but a certain sort and degree of motion in the minute particles of our nerves or animal spirits, we may understand how it is possible that the same water may, at the same time, produce the sensations of heat in one hand and cold in the other; which yet figure never does, that never producing- the idea of a square by one hand which has produced the idea of a globe by another. But if the sensation of heat and cold be nothing but the increase or diminution of the motion of the minute parts of our bodies, caused by the corpuscles of any other body, it is easy to be understood, that if that motion be greater in one hand than in the other; if a body be applied to the two hands, which has in its minute particles a greater motion than in those of one of the hands, and a less than in those of the other, it will increase the motion of the one hand and lessen it in the other; and so cause the different sensations of heat and cold that depend thereon.

22. An excursion into natural philosophy. I have in what just goes before been engaged in physical inquiries a little further than perhaps I intended. But, it being necessary to make the nature of sensation a little understood; and to make the difference between the qualities in bodies, and the ideas produced by them in the mind, to be distinctly conceived, without which it were impossible to discourse intelligibly of them;- I hope I shall be pardoned this little excursion into natural philosophy; it being necessary in our present inquiry to distinguish the primary and real qualities of bodies, which are always in them (viz. solidity, extension, figure, number, and motion, or rest, and are sometimes perceived by us, viz. when the bodies they are in are big enough singly to be discerned), from those secondary and imputed qualities, which are but the powers of several combinations of those primary ones, when they operate without being distinctly discerned;- whereby we may also come to know what ideas are, and what are not, resemblances of something really existing in the bodies we denominate from them.

23. Three sorts of qualities in bodies. The qualities, then, that are in bodies, rightly considered, are of three sorts:-

First, The bulk, figure, number, situation, and motion or rest of their solid parts. Those are in them, whether we perceive them or not; and when they are of that size that we can discover them, we have by these an idea of the thing as it is in itself; as is plain in artificial things. These I call primary qualities.

Secondly, The power that is in any body, by reason of its insensible primary qualities, to operate after a peculiar manner on any of our senses, and thereby produce in us the different ideas of several colours, sounds, smells, tastes, &c. These are usually called sensible qualities.

Thirdly, The power that is in any body, by reason of the particular constitution of its primary qualities, to make such a change in the bulk, figure, texture, and motion of another body, as to make it operate on our senses differently from what it did before. Thus the sun has a power to make wax white, and fire to make lead fluid. These are usually called powers.

The first of these, as has been said, I think may be properly called real, original, or primary qualities; because they are in the things themselves, whether they are perceived or not: and upon their different modifications it is that the secondary qualities depend.

The other two are only powers to act differently upon other things: which powers result from the different modifications of those primary qualities.

24. The first are resemblances; the second thought to be resemblances, but are not; the third neither are nor are thought so. But, though the two latter sorts of qualities are powers barely, and nothing but powers, relating to several other bodies, and resulting from the different modifications of the original qualities, yet they are generally otherwise thought of. For the second sort, viz, the powers to produce several ideas in us, by our senses, are looked upon as real qualities in the things thus affecting us: but the third sort are called and esteemed barely powers. v.g. The idea of heat or light, which we receive by our eyes, or touch, from the sun, are commonly thought real qualities existing in the sun, and something more than mere powers in it. But when we consider the sun in reference to wax, which it melts or blanches, we look on the whiteness and softness produced in the wax, not as qualities in the sun, but effects produced by powers in it. Whereas, if rightly considered, these qualities of light and warmth, which are perceptions in me when I am warmed or enlightened by the sun, are no otherwise in the sun, than the changes made in the wax, when it is blanched or melted, are in the sun. They are all of them equally powers in the sun, depending on its primary qualities; whereby it is able, in the one case, so to alter the bulk, figure, texture, or motion of some of the insensible parts of my eyes or hands, as thereby to produce in me the idea of light or heat; and in the other, it is able so to alter the bulk, figure, texture, or motion of the insensible parts of the wax, as to make them fit to produce in me the distinct ideas of white and fluid.

25. Why the secondary are ordinarily taken for real qualities, and not for bare powers. The reason why the one are ordinarily taken for real qualities, and the other only for bare powers, seems to be, because the ideas we have of distinct colours, sounds, &c., containing nothing at all in them of bulk, figure, or motion, we are not apt to think them the effects of these primary qualities; which appear not, to our senses, to operate in their production, and with which they have not any apparent congruity or conceivable connection. Hence it is that we

are so forward to imagine, that those ideas are the resemblances of something really existing in the objects themselves: since sensation discovers nothing of bulk, figure, or motion of parts in their production; nor can reason show how bodies, by their bulk, figure, and motion, should produce in the mind the ideas of blue or yellow, &c. But, in the other case, in the operations of bodies changing the qualities one of another, we plainly discover that the quality produced hath commonly no resemblance with anything in the thing producing it; wherefore we look on it as a bare effect of power. For, through receiving the idea of heat or light from the sun, we are apt to think it is a perception and resemblance of such a quality in the sun; yet when we see wax, or a fair face, receive change of colour from the sun, we cannot imagine that to be the reception or resemblance of anything in the sun, because we find not those different colours in the sun itself. For, our senses being able to observe a likeness or unlikeness of sensible qualities in two different external objects, we forwardly enough conclude the production of any sensible quality in any subject to be an effect of bare power, and not the communication of any quality which was really in the efficient, when we find no such sensible quality in the thing that produced it. But our senses, not being able to discover any unlikeness between the idea produced in us, and the quality of the object producing it, we are apt to imagine that our ideas are resemblances of something in the objects, and not the effects of certain powers placed in the modification of their primary qualities, with which primary qualities the ideas produced in us have no resemblance.

26. Secondary qualities twofold; first, immediately perceivable; secondly, mediately perceivable. To conclude. Besides those before-mentioned primary qualities in bodies, viz. bulk, figure, extension, number, and motion of their solid parts; all the rest, whereby we take notice of bodies, and distinguish them one from another, are nothing else but several powers in them, depending on those primary qualities; whereby they are fitted, either by immediately operating on our bodies to produce several different ideas in us; or else, by operating on other bodies, so to change their primary qualities as to render them capable of producing ideas in us different from what before they did. The former of these, I think, may be called secondary

qualities immediately perceivable: the latter, secondary qualities, mediately perceivable.

Of Complex Ideas

1. Made by the mind out of simple ones. We have hitherto considered those ideas, in the reception whereof the mind is only passive, which are those simple ones received from sensation and reflection before mentioned, whereof the mind cannot make one to itself, nor have any idea which does not wholly consist of them. But as the mind is wholly passive in the reception of all its simple ideas, so it exerts several acts of its own, whereby out of its simple ideas, as the materials and foundations of the rest, the others are framed. The acts of the mind, wherein it exerts its power over its simple ideas, are chiefly these three: (1) Combining several simple ideas into one compound one; and thus all complex ideas are made. (2) The second is bringing two ideas, whether simple or complex, together, and setting them by one another, so as to take a view of them at once, without uniting them into one; by which way it gets all its ideas of relations. (3) The third is separating them from all other ideas that accompany them in their real existence: this is called abstraction: and thus all its general ideas are made. This shows man's power, and its ways of operation, to be much the same in the material and intellectual world. For the materials in both being such as he has no power over, either to make or destroy, all that man can do is either to unite them together, or to set them by one another, or wholly separate them. I shall here begin with the first of these in the consideration of complex ideas, and come to the other two in their due places. As simple ideas are observed to exist in several combinations united together, so the mind has a power to consider several of them united together as one idea; and that not only as they are united in external objects, but as itself has joined them together. Ideas thus made up of several simple ones put together, I call complex;- such as are beauty, gratitude, a man, an army, the universe; which, though complicated of various simple ideas, or complex ideas made up of simple ones, yet are, when the mind pleases, considered each by itself, as one entire thing, and signified by one name.

2. Made voluntarily. In this faculty of repeating and joining together its ideas, the mind has great power in varying and multiplying the objects of its thoughts, infinitely beyond what sensation or reflection furnished it with: but all this still confined to those simple

ideas which it received from those two sources, and which are the ultimate materials of all its compositions. For simple ideas are all from things themselves, and of these the mind can have no more, nor other than what are suggested to it. It can have no other ideas of sensible qualities than what come from without by the senses; nor any ideas of other kind of operations of a thinking substance, than what it finds in itself But when it has once got these simple ideas, it is not confined barely to observation, and what offers itself from without; it can, by its own power, put together those ideas it has, and make new complex ones, which it never received so united.

3. Complex ideas are either of modes, substances, or relations. Complex ideas, however compounded and decompounded, though their number be infinite, and the variety endless, wherewith they fill and entertain the thoughts of men; yet I think they may be all reduced under these three heads:-

1. Modes.
2. Substances.
3. Relations.

4. Ideas of modes. First, Modes I call such complex ideas which, however compounded, contain not in them the supposition of subsisting by themselves, but are considered as dependencies on, or affections of substances;- such as are the ideas signified by the words triangle, gratitude, murder, &c. And if in this I use the word mode in somewhat a different sense from its ordinary signification, I beg pardon; it being unavoidable in discourses, differing from the ordinary received notions, either to make new words, or to use old words in somewhat a new signification; the later whereof, in our present case, is perhaps the more tolerable of the two.

5. Simple and mixed modes of simple ideas. Of these modes, there are two sorts which deserve distinct consideration:

First, there are some which are only variations, or different combinations of the same simple idea, without the mixture of any other;- as a dozen, or score; which are nothing but the ideas of so many distinct units added together, and these I call simple modes as being contained within the bounds of one simple idea.

Secondly, there are others compounded of simple ideas of several kinds, put together to make one complex one;- v.g. beauty, consisting of a certain composition of colour and figure, causing delight to the beholder; theft, which being the concealed change of the possession of anything, without the consent of the proprietor, contains, as is visible, a combination of several ideas of several kinds: and these I call mixed modes.

6. Ideas of substances, single or collective. Secondly, the ideas of Substances are such combinations of simple ideas as are taken to represent distinct particular things subsisting by themselves; the supposed or confused idea of substance, such as it is, is always the first and chief Thus if to substance be joined the simple idea of a certain dull whitish colour, with certain degrees of weight, hardness, ductility, and fusibility, we have the idea of lead; and a combination of the ideas of a certain sort of figure, with the powers of motion, thought and reasoning, joined to substance, the ordinary idea of a man. Now of substances also, there are two sorts of ideas:- one of single substances, as they exist separately, as of a man or a sheep; the other of several of those put together, as an army of men, or flock of sheep- which collective ideas of several substances thus put together are as much each of them one single idea as that of a man or an unit.

7. Ideas of relation. Thirdly, the last sort of complex ideas is that we call Relation, which consists in the consideration and comparing one idea with another.

Of these several kinds we shall treat in their order.

8. The abstrusest ideas we can have are all from two sources. If we trace the progress of our minds, and with attention observe how it repeats, adds together, and unites its simple ideas received from sensation or reflection, it will lead us further than at first perhaps we should have imagined. And, I believe, we shall find, if we warily observe the originals of our notions, that even the most abstruse ideas, how remote soever they may seem from sense, or from any operations of our own minds, are yet only such as the understanding frames to itself, by repeating and joining together ideas that it had either from objects of sense, or from its own operations about them: so that those even large and abstract ideas are derived from sensation or reflection, being no other than what the mind, by the ordinary use of its own faculties, employed about ideas received from objects of sense, or from the operations it observes in itself about them, may, and does, attain unto.

This I shall endeavour to show in the ideas we have of space, time, and infinity, and some few others that seem the most remote, from those originals.

PRINCIPAL WORKS OF LOCKE

Essay Concerning Human Understanding, 1690
Two Treatises of Government, 1690
Letter Concerning Toleration, 1689
Some Thoughts Concerning Education, 1693